COLORADO

COLORADO

A SUMMER TRIP

BY

BAYARD TAYLOR

Edited by William W. Savage, Jr.
and
James H. Lazalier

UNIVERSITY PRESS OF COLORADO

Copyright © 1989 by the University Press of Colorado, Niwot, Colorado 80544

The University Press of Colorado is a cooperative publishing enterprise supported, in part, by Adams State College, Colorado State University, Fort Lewis College, Mesa State College, Metropolitan State College, University of Colorado, University of Northern Colorado, University of Southern Colorado, and Western State College.

The paper used in this publication meets the minimum requirements of the American National Standard for Information Sciences — Permanence of Paper for Printed Library Materials, ANSI Z39.48–1984.

Library of Congress Cataloging-in-Publication Data

Taylor, Bayard, 1825–1878.
    Colorado: a summer trip / by Bayard Taylor; edited by William W. Savage, Jr. and James H. Lazalier.
        p.   cm.
    Reprint. Originally published: New York: Putnam, 1867.
    ISBN 0-87081-182-7 — ISBN 0-87081-177-0 (pbk.)
    1. Colorado—Description and travel—To 1876. 2. Taylor, Bayard, 1825–1878—Journeys—Colorado. 3. Taylor, Bayard, 1825–1878—Correspondence. I. Savage, William W. II. Lazalier, James H. III. Title.
F780.T38 1989
917.8804'2—dc20

THESE letters, originally published in the *New York Tribune*, are reproduced in this form, in order to meet the demands of a general interest in the regions they describe.

CONTENTS

INTRODUCTION

BY WILLIAM W. SAVAGE, JR. AND JAMES H. LAZALIER

BAYARD TAYLOR (1825–1878) was surely the best-known traveler of his day. He preferred to think of himself as a poet and a novelist; and he expected to be remembered for the quality of his verse. But his travel writing initiated and sustained his literary career and became his only enduring legacy. In *Colorado: A Summer Trip*, an account of his western travels during June and July of 1866, we have a small example of the best of it.

A Pennsylvania-born son of a farmer-cum-sheriff, Bayard Taylor decided early on to abandon the land to siblings and seek his fortune in proximity to a printing press. Journalism seemed to beckon, but he found the work irregular. Without money to further his education, he apprenticed himself to a printer and tried producing his own collections of poetry, available to patrons of the arts by subscription only. If that were not a clearly marked literary dead-end, it seemed close enough for fiscal discomfort; so Taylor bought up his apprenticeship and launched a new career that would bring him to national prominence in remarkably short order.

At the age of nineteen, Taylor managed to bankroll a trip to Europe by securing advances from such publications as *Saturday Evening Post* and Horace Greeley's *New York Tribune* for a series of letters he proposed to send back recounting his adventures abroad. The experience was to be for Taylor the equivalent of a college education, albeit one acquired on a shoestring. His travels took him to England, Germany, Austria, Italy, and France, and through two years of his life. It was a walking tour; and it carried Taylor away from the beaten path, in search of affordable accommodations. Going the odd way to strange places allowed Taylor to report on matters that came as news to cognoscenti. His youth was an obvious asset (though at first it must not have seemed so to his editors), contributing both enthusiasm and a fresh perspective. The mixture worked: Taylor's letters were enormously popular, and so was the book he made of them in 1846.[1]

During the next dozen years, Taylor journeyed to California at Greeley's request (before he cribbed "Go west, young man" from John Babson Lane Soul) to view the gold rush; to central Africa and the region of the White Nile; to Palestine, Asia Minor, Sicily, and Spain; to China and thence, with Matthew C. Perry, to the opening of Japan; to the Scandinavian countries; to Crete, Greece, and Russia. Among the reading public, he became known as the "Great American Traveler," a cognomen he abhorred as unfit for a man of letters — especially for the man of letters he supposed himself to be. But the pattern of travel was firmly set, and Taylor would not be able to break it. Travel writing was his forte. Moreover, it was what his public expected; and, for his part, with bills to pay, Taylor could find no more lucrative literary pastime.

Taylor learned early in the game to exploit each trip at least three times. First, he sold the letters his travels spawned to newspapers and magazines. Later, he published the letters in book form. Finally, he sifted and refined the material for presentation on the lecture circuit. Taylor was a keen observer and a facile writer and thus could interest publishers and sustain an audience in the great age of the armchair traveler, when sedentary Americans preferred to let somebody else enjoy the infelicities of daily existence in remote and exotic locales. Over the years, Taylor's travel writing proved to be his only reliable source of income (aside from occasional employment as a salaried journalist), and he used it to buy time for the pursuit of what he considered his substantial interests, including a long-term project — the translation of Goethe's Faust.[2] The desire for a revenue-producing holiday from this particular unpaid chore (he was trying for English rhymes with the meter of the German) took Taylor to Colorado in 1866.

Bayard Taylor would have preferred not to travel — or at least not to be obliged to write about it. Ideally he wanted a sinecure, a government post of some sort, to bring economic stability to his life and finance his serious work. In 1878, he received appointment as minister to Germany. Taylor was, of course, delighted. The post was perfect for a Germanophile with plans for a biography of Goethe; but as it happened, he would not live to enjoy it. Too much travel and too much writing — fifty books in his fifty-three years, together with hundreds if not thousands of periodical publications, to say nothing of better than twenty-thousand known letters — had taken their toll. And, to be candid about it, there had been entirely too much liquor along the way. Taylor drank like a fish, praising all the while the abundant virtues of alcohol for a man of letters. (It was also an essential item of the traveler's baggage, a nostrum for the ills of the road.) In any event, his health was broken, and he died after only a few months in Germany. His obituary in the *New York Times* reported that his passing was "peaceful and painless," but in view of the important work he thought he was leaving unfinished, it could not have been.[3]

Modern biographers, perhaps drawn to Taylor initially by the phenomenon of his sudden rise to literary prominence, seem compelled to account for the equally meteoric decline in his popularity, a long slide toward literary oblivion to be curbed at last by neither the quality nor the quantity of his work. To Richmond Croom Beatty, Taylor was "laureate of the Gilded Age" only because he was a prisoner of the times, unable to reach beyond the shallow conventions of his day to speak meaningfully to us in ours.[4] Others have suggested that Taylor was the eventual victim of his own bloated opinion of his writing. Editors seldom if ever rejected anything Taylor sent them because if he and they were not already close personal friends, each knew somebody who knew the other.[5] Therefore, he received kid-glove treatment when his work deserved vigorous application of the blue pencil; and because of that, Taylor came to think of his literary efforts as uniformly good. According to this theory, Taylor may have been a posthumous victim of changing taste; but he was also laid even lower in the century after his death by a fraternity of critics recanting the overblown compliments of his pals, their predecessors.[6] All of that may be true enough with regard to his poetry and fiction; but the same brush should not tar his travel writing. It is different stuff and deserves a different sort of consideration.

Bayard Taylor was a mediocre novelist and a worse poet, to whom the word saccharine cannot begin to do justice.[7] As a translator, his greatest achievement was to turn Goethe's *Faust* into fairly bad English verse, although he did it largely from memory, and that was impressive.[8] In contrast, the travel narratives sparkle with verve and gusto, even when Taylor claimed to be thoroughly jaded by the experiences that yielded them.

Frivolous and altogether ephemeral he may have thought
them to be, the travel books were not without value
beyond the immediate gratification of Taylor's devoted
following. They encapsulate place and time for the modern reader and thus they are history; but still they couch
Taylor's observations in a style so crisp and fresh that it
hardly smacks of the nineteenth century at all. As the fate
of Ozymandias demonstrated to Shelley's satisfaction, a
man may not know which of his works will survive; but in
Taylor's case, if anything calls to question his literary
judgment, it must be his own denigration of the travel
books and his apparent misunderstanding of the merits
of his observations of diverse parts of the globe.

Colorado: A Summer Trip is casually dismissed by most of
Taylor's biographers as a minor work — not even a thing
to be damned by faint praise.[9] Specialists in Western
Americana have not exactly ignored the book, but neither
have they rushed forward to tout its utility.[10] One modern critic has had the temerity to call it "a classic of
American overland adventure," but similar assessments
are few and far between.[11] Nevertheless, there is much
in Taylor's little book to recommend it and certainly to
justify its reconsideration.

First, *Colorado: A Summer Trip* offers insight into Taylor's
travel-narrative procedures. This book fits the classic
Taylor mold. Its genesis is to be found in letters to
Greeley's *Tribune*; and although we have his wife's testimony to the effect that recreation, not remuneration,
provided the motive for the journey,[12] it is clear that he
approached the experience as an occasion for profit.
Vacation or not, it led first to letters and then to the book;
and Taylor admitted throughout the account to lecturing
at every opportunity. That, together with his frequent
comments upon the price of western food, lodging, and
transportation, may indicate the extent to which money
(or his lack of it) occupied his mind. Add to that the

strenuous nature of his Colorado travels — something that could not fail to appeal to armchair adventurers — and we have a picture, not of a literary figure off to banish care with a bit of rustic relaxation, but of a professional travel writer plying his trade. The only respite Taylor found in Colorado was from his hard work on *Faust* and the contemplation of his next novel.

Then there are Taylor's descriptions and asides. The land was explained, the people described, their economies limned; and relevant comparisons were made, drawn from Taylor's extensive inventory of places previously considered. Beyond that, he touched upon any number of fascinating topics: the Great American Desert of Stephen Long's imaginings, the persistence of the myth, and the need for a certificate of its death to verify what anyone could plainly see; the possible routes of the Union Pacific Railroad then under construction and what that marvel would mean to the development of the West; and Colorado's impending designation as America's Switzerland, with all that such a label implied. The book's title suggests the mundane, but nothing refracted by the lens of Taylor's practical eye could remain the slightest bit prosaic: A little girl before a dugout, claiming to need no doll since prairie dogs and horses were better playmates, becomes a figure to arrest attention — first Taylor's, then ours; and owing to such magic we allow ourselves to follow where he goes.

Taylor's account stands as a world-class observer's first-class treatment of territory that few were competing to present to a literate and sophisticated constituency. He visited Colorado at a time when the mining industry was in hiatus. Lesser men might have bemoaned their bad luck, but Taylor took things as he found them; and here was a chance to see the place less cluttered with the distractions of economic boom than it might otherwise have been — cluttered by the miners, that is. Their earlier ravages upon the land were only too evident. Indeed, Taylor preferred a West without white men scrambling over every rock and splashing through each rill in search of precious metal or anything else. He supposed that Colorado would be open to "general travel" as early as 1868 and accessible by rail from New York City for any with the money and four days to invest in travel time. Civilization loomed just over the horizon, as it were. "Therefore, I am doubly glad that I have come *now*," he wrote, "while there are still buffaloes and danger of Indians on the Plains, camp-fires to build in the mountains, rivers to swim, and landscapes to enjoy, which have never yet been described."[13] In effect, Taylor offered history before it was too late.

The frontier and the prospect of its passing were clearly of some interest to Taylor, who in his time had seen more wildernesses than one. The Great American Desert, comparison informed him, was hardly that at all; and comparison taught other lessons as well. In Colorado, Taylor saw something of the frontier as process, as suggested by this passage:

> The degree of refinement which I have found in the remote mining districts of Colorado has been a great surprise. California, after ten years' settlement, retained a proportion of the rough, original mining element; but Montana has acted as a social *strainer* to Colorado; or, rather, as a miner's pan, shaking out a vast deal of dirt and leaving the gold behind. Mr. Leonhardy and his neighbors live in rude cabins, but they do not therefore relinquish the the graces of life. It is only the *half*-cultivated who, under such circumstances, relapse toward barbarism. Mountain life soon rubs off the veneering, and we know of what wood men are made.[14]

Here, by three decades, Bayard Taylor both anticipated and refuted some of the pronouncements of Frederick Jackson Turner, the historian who invented the frontier as an academic pastime. In his 1893 essay, "The Significance of the Frontier in American History," Turner argued that "at the frontier the environment is at first too strong for the man," overwhelming the European colonist and reducing him to the level of the Indian (an animal, to Turner, an item of fauna), before allowing him back up the ladder of civilization, rung by rung, to emerge, not as the European he had been at the beginning of the process, but as "a new product that is American."[15] Taylor, who had seen more of the world than Turner ever would, could not have accepted such a notion. In his experience, a gentleman remained a gentleman despite the frontier. Only one who was a rude fellow to start with would be adversely affected by frontier influence. Economic booms might lure a bum from one kind of frontier to another, but a bum he would remain, regardless of remote venue. It was Charles Darwin's wisdom that an organism in any environment had but three choices: move, adapt, or die. Turner would judge adaptation to be the principal characteristic of the westering American, but in 1866 Taylor argued for the subversion of the entire process.[16] Ruffians moved, feeling no compulsion to adapt — or to adapt further — to circumstances already so central to their status as riffraff. Gentlemen, in contrast, neither succumbed to Nature nor adapted to it, nor were they provoked to move. It was as if wilderness made way for gentlemen. Ruffians might make their own way, but to nobody's great advantage and certainly not to civilization's. Neither class contributed to the passing of the frontier, in Taylor's view: not gentlemen, because they made no alteration of the environment; and not ruffians, because they always went quickly off in pursuit of the next thing. On the contrary, the railroad, steady and mechanical, would mark the end of the frontier, overwhelming it with sheer numbers of immigrants willing to make the trip.

Turner resided near the frontier during his formative years. It is perhaps worth noting that the tranquil, nearly genteel frontier Taylor saw during the summer of 1866 bore little resemblance to the boisterous and sometimes violent one observed that same summer by five-year-old Fred Turner, romping in the dusty streets of Portage, Wisconsin.[17] Perhaps Taylor was too jaded to notice any real unpleasantness, or perhaps he did not care to offend his readers by remarking upon it. Whatever the case, not even a stagecoach ride with the notorious John M. Chivington, responsible for the Sand Creek Massacre of hundreds of Cheyenne men, women, and children in 1864, could move Taylor to a recitation of blood-and-thunder yarns about the West. If they discussed more than the railroad's progress, Taylor did not report it. Nor did the Indians Taylor encountered afford many possibilities. As he told his wife, they were all friendly.[18]

Something should be said of Bayard Taylor's principal companions during his weeks in Colorado. The "Mr. Beard" of the text was William Holbrook Beard (1824–1900), one of the noted artists of the day. He was, by all accounts, along to paint landscapes, although nobody nowadays seems to know whatever became of his Colorado pictures. They were not included in Taylor's book, and while some claimed to have seen them (Taylor could hardly have missed them), their whereabouts remain a minor mystery.[19]

By 1866, Beard's reputation rested largely on his talents as a painter of anthropomorphic animals, a line of work to which he had turned as a failed portraitist and in which he seemed inextricably mired whenever it came to making money.[20] As an artist who wished to be known for something other than what he did best, he had much in common with the Great American Traveler. The two men were entirely different physical specimens, however. Nine months Taylor's senior, Beard offered no match for the writer's stamina; and the business of packing canvas and brushes on horseback through the wilderness appears to have worn him to a frazzle. "Poor Beard," Taylor wrote his wife after one of their adventures, "is used up — he can't even sketch."[21] Perhaps the contentious Arapaho mare, of which Taylor so often complained, had helped to rattle the artist, troubling his mind with visions of anthropomorphic demon-horses.

The expert mountaineer and the party's guide through the Colorado outback was William Newton Byers (1831–1903), editor and publisher of the *Rocky Mountain News*.[22] Byers had arrived in Denver from Omaha during the gold rush of 1859 with a wagonload of printing equipment; had established his shop on an upper floor of a saloon operated by legendary mountain man and Indian fighter Richens Lacy "Uncle Dick" Wootton; and had beaten the competition to produce the first newspaper in Colorado by just about twenty minutes. At a time when eastern papers sold for a penny or two or three, Byers had charged twenty-five cents for his sheet, owing to the expense of having national and international news reports brought by messenger from the Fort Laramie post office — the nearest one, but still some 225 miles away. Soon enough, Denver obtained its own post office; and in 1866 Byers was serving as the city's postmaster. An indefatigable booster of Colorado's political fortunes, he was also during that year involved in one of a continuing series of attempts by locals to attain statehood for the territory. Doubtless he told Bayard Taylor everything he needed to know about the bright and shining future of America's Switzerland.

It was Byers the outdoorsman, not "poor Beard" or the stout and tippling Taylor, who was nearly drowned beneath the icy waters of the Blue River when his horse lost its footing and was swept downstream.[23] Taylor counted himself fortunate to have avoided a similar mishap. The fact was that Taylor, who had circled the globe en route to visiting every place worth seeing and more than a few that were not, had never experienced greater difficulty in getting about than he had in Colorado. "I never knew what rough travel was, before," he confided in a letter to his wife.[24] If Byers, with all his skill, had been lucky to survive the Blue River, then Taylor must have felt positively blessed to be able to make it back to Pennsylvania.

Bayard Taylor was a better travel writer than most of his contemporaries and his immediate heirs. If we eliminate Mark Twain's *Roughing It* (1872) as something more — and less — than a travel book, we still find Taylor's Western efforts superior to such items as Horace Greeley's *An Overland Journey from New York to San Francisco in the Summer of 1859* (1860), a useful volume for comparison, since Greeley, too, visited Colorado. Greeley's newspaper background might excuse his tendency to pontificate — he wrote his own editorials, remember, and he had plenty of opinions, especially where the West was concerned. But we know that Taylor had a similar background. Indeed, he was often Greeley's employee, and when he was, he wrote the *Tribune* editorials when Greeley was otherwise occupied.[25] Yet, the drum Taylor beat in his book was a snare in counterpoint to Greeley's timpani. Greeley, for example, held that there was no hope for the Indian, an impediment, after all, to the progress of white settlers whose homesteads were a favorite Greeley cause. Indeed, the development of the West, generally, seemed a Greeley obsession.[26] Taylor hoped to see things and report them before development arrived; and he never met an Indian he could not tolerate.[27]

Colorado: A Summer Trip is far more insightful, thought-
ful, and judicious (to say nothing of fair) than Richard
Harding Davis's *The West from a Car-Window* (1892), which
is taken to be thoroughly representative of nineteenth-
century journalistic travel writing. Davis affected a snobbish, condescending manner. An unrepentant eastern
elitist, he believed — and frequently asserted — that any
man would be better off as a peon in the poorest and
lowliest of New York slums than he would be as a prince
in some rowdy western backwater.[28] For all he saw of the
West, Davis might as well never have climbed off the
train. For all that he understood of the West, some would
argue that he never did.[29] About Bayard Taylor, aboard
his sore-footed Indian pony, we have considerably fewer
doubts. Unlike Davis, who seldom if ever knew whereof
he spoke, Taylor knew almost exactly, and him we gladly
embrace as the reliable guide.

A hundred years ago, a Bayard Taylor travel book
could be counted upon to provide a good read. That is
no less true today. *Colorado: A Summer Trip* is a zesty morsel
of history, and for the modern Coloradan a word-portrait
of yesteryear, a useful reminder of the origins called
heritage. It is worthwhile, as well, as an example from a
rich tradition of travel literature, a forebear of the con-
tributions of Burton Holmes, Lowell Thomas, Harry
Franck, and Richard Halliburton — a form of diversion
rendered quaint these days by the cavalier meanderings
of television and sustained in print only by *National Geo-
graphic* and the occasional railroad opus of Paul Theroux.
Because he was good at it, Taylor deserves an evening
and the chance to take us elsewhere.

NOTES

The text of *Colorado: A Summer Trip* is reproduced from the edition published in New York by G. P. Putnam and Son in January 1867.

1. Bayard Taylor, *Views Afoot; or Europe Seen with Knapsack and Staff* (New York: Wiley & Putnam, 1846). Much was made of the fact that young Taylor's version of the Grand Tour was accomplished at a cost of only $500, when the high-falutin' might reasonably expect to pay a minimum of $5,000. See also Sharon Ann Tumulty, "From Persia to Peoria: Bayard Taylor as Travel Writer," Ph.D. dissertation, University of Delaware, 1971.

2. William Charvat has referred to the "false dualism" of Taylor and other young writers of his day. It grew from "subsidizing their unprofitable 'art' by grinding out commercially successful work of which they were contemptuous." Indeed, Taylor was Charvat's primary example: "Bayard Taylor was humiliated that on his lecture tours women swooned, and cried, 'There he is! That's him!' And he complained that lecturing, which built him a fifteen-thousand-dollar country house, was destroying his poetry, which he never wrote for money." Charvat, "The People's Patronage," in Robert E. Spiller, Willard Thorp, et al. (eds.), *Literary History of the United States: History*, 3d ed. (New York: The Macmillan Company, 1963), p. 524.

3. New York *Times*, December 20, 1878, p. 1.

4. Richmond Croom Beatty, *Bayard Taylor: Laureate of the Gilded Age* (Norman: University of Oklahoma Press, 1936).

5. When P. T. Barnum brought Jenny Lind to New York, there was the predictable ballyhoo of a contest to see who could write the best song for her to sing, and Bayard Taylor won it. Taylor "gave the number of disappointed entrants as 752; and he probably knew, for his publisher

and his editorial associate on the *Tribune* were two of the three members of the Committee" that awarded the $200 prize. E. Douglas Branch, *The Sentimental Years, 1836–1860* (New York: D. Appleton-Century Company, 1934), p. 187. Thus was Taylor accustomed to acceptance. This sort of thing only encouraged him.

6. See the discussion in Paul C. Wermuth, *Bayard Taylor* (New York: Twayne Publishers, Inc., 1973), pp. 177–79. See also Richard Cary, *The Genteel Circle: Bayard Taylor and His New York Friends* (Ithaca: Cornell University Press, 1952).

7. Any assertion about the quality of Taylor's "serious" literary efforts need only be supported by a verse or two of his most famous ode, "Bedouin Song" (1853):

> From the Desert I come to thee,
> On a stallion shod with fire,
> And the winds are left behind
> In the speed of my desire.
> Under thy window I stand,
> And the midnight hears my cry.
> I love thee, I love but thee,
> With a love that never shall die,
>   *Till the sun grows cold,*
>   *And the stars are old,*
>   *And the leaves of the Judgment Book unfold!*

(Not that rotten poetry was contagious or anything, but on the occasion of Taylor's death, Henry Wadsworth Longfellow really did write this:

> Dead he lay among his books!
> The peace of God was in his looks.

Several critics have contended that Taylor's inspiration
for "Bedouin Song" was Percy Shelley's "The Indian
Serenade" (1822), the first verse of which reads this way:

> I arise from dreams of thee
> In the first sweet sleep of night,
> When the winds are breathing low,
> And the stars are shining bright:
> I arise from dreams of thee,
> And a spirit in my feet
> Hath led me — who knows how?
> To thy chamber window, Sweet!

Well, at least Taylor's bedouin owned a horse. Charitab-
ly, Fred Lewis Pattee, in his *Century Readings in American
Literature* (4th ed., New York: The Century Co., 1932),
p. 709, explained the similarity with Shelley this way:
"Taylor's phenomenal memory was stocked with the
poetry of all the world and he wrote, unconsciously
doubtless, always from a recollection of this storehouse
rather than from a driving creative impulse that sent
him into fields new and strange." We conclude, then,
that the very thing which embued his travel writing was
entirely absent from his poetry, and that Taylor never
knew it.

8. Taylor was non-resident professor of German literature
at Cornell University, 1870–1877, an appointment
made on the basis of the appearance of the first volume
of his *Faust* in 1870.

9. See Albert H. Smyth, *Bayard Taylor* (Boston: Houghton,
Mifflin and Company, 1896), p. 178, for a typical example. Beatty, *Bayard Taylor*, did not mention either the
trip or the book, although he listed the book in Taylor's
bibliography.

10. Walter S. Campbell (Stanley Vestal), *The Book Lover's Southwest: A Guide to Good Reading* (Norman: University of Oklahoma Press, 1955), p. 57, illustrates the point. *Colorado: A Summer Trip* must be "good reading" because it is included in the guide; but Campbell gave no idea of its content and could not therefore justify its inclusion. Some historians of the mining frontier have found Taylor's descriptions of California and Colorado useful for providing touches of local color, e.g., William S. Greever, *The Bonanza West: The Story of the Western Mining Rushes, 1848–1900* (Norman: University of Oklahoma Press, 1963).

11. The phrase belongs to James A. Levernier, in Taylor's entry in *American Literature to 1900* (New York: St. Martin's Press, 1980), p. 280; but Levernier also believed that Horace Greeley published the *New York Times*.

12. Marie Hansen Taylor, with Lilian Bayard Taylor Kiliani, *On Two Continents: Memories of Half a Century* (New York: Doubleday, Page & Company, 1905), p. 165.

13. Below, p. 166.

14. Below, p. 131. The Colorado rush of 1859 followed a gold strike in 1858. Strikes in Montana occurred in 1862, 1863, 1864, and 1865.

15. Frederick Jackson Turner, "The Significance of the Frontier in American History," in Turner, *The Frontier in American History* (New York: Holt, Rinehart and Winston, Inc., 1920), p. 4.

16. Taylor read Darwin five years after his trip to Colorado. Turner read Darwin ten years before expounding his ideas on the form and function of frontiers. Smyth, *Bayard Taylor*, p. 231; Ray Allen Billington, *Frederick Jackson Turner: Historian, Scholar, Teacher* (New York: Oxford University Press, 1973), pp. 30–31.

17. *Ibid.*, p. 15.

18. Below, p. 174; Taylor, with Kiliani, *On Two Continents,* p. 169.

19. Robert Taft, *Artists and Illustrators of the Old West, 1850 –1900* (New York: Charles Scribner's Sons, 1953), p. 57.

20. *Ibid.*, p. 295.

21. Taylor, with Kiliani, *On Two Continents,* op. cit.

22. See Maxine Benson's article on Byers in Howard R. Lamar (ed.), *The Reader's Encyclopedia of the American West* (New York: Thomas Y. Crowell Company, 1977), pp. 144–45.

23. And Byers was *tough.* See Greever, *Bonanza West*, p. 169.

24. Taylor, with Kiliani, *On Two Continents,* op. cit.

25. John Tebbel, *The Media in America* (New York: Thomas Y. Crowell Company, 1974), p. 173.

26. "Those people," Greeley wrote of the Indians in 1859, "must die out — there is no help for them. God has given this earth to those who will subdue and cultivate it, and it is vain to struggle against His righteous decree." He wrote worse things, too, in that same letter. He drafted it in Denver on June 16, 1859, and it was published in the *Tribune* under the title "Lo! The Poor Indian!" See Horace Greeley, *An Overland Journey from New York to San Fransico in the Summer of 1859*, ed. by Charles T. Duncan (New York: Alfred A. Knopf, 1964), p. 120. Of course, Indian-thumping, satisfied *Tribune* subscribers and, as Taylor once noted, the *Tribune* followed only the Bible as favored reading matter in the West. In any case, Greeley's remarks anticipated (though without the humor) Twain's in *Roughing It*. See p. 146 of *The Works of Mark Twain*, vol. 2 (Berkeley: University of California Press, 1972).

27. But there were some he did not meet. See below, p. 23.

28. When Davis visited Creede, Colorado, he heard of G. L. Smith's refusal to take $1,250,000 for his share of the

Holy Moses Mine. "After that my interest in him fell away," he wrote. "Any man who will live in a log house at the foot of a mountain, and drink melted snow any longer than he has to do so, or refuse that much money for *anything*, when he could live in the Knickerbocker Flats, and drive forth in a private hansom with rubber tires, is no longer an object of public interest." Later, in Oklahoma City, he expressed the opinion that "any man who can afford a hall bedroom and a gas-stove in New York City is better off than he would be as the owner of one hundred and sixty acres on the prairie, or in one of these small so-called cities." See Richard Harding Davis, *The West from a Car-Window* (New York: Harper & Brothers, 1892), pp. 68, 114. For an interesting Colorado contrast, compare Davis's third chapter, "At a New Mining Camp," with Taylor's ninth chapter, "Mining and Mining Processes," below.

29. One of the people Davis saw in action in Creede was William Barclay Masterson of Dodge, Tombstone, and other places. Masterson may or may not have been a peace officer in Creede in 1892, but Davis found him dealing cards in a saloon, heard he had killed some twenty-eight men, and then proceeded to write of him as "Bat Masterden." See Davis, *West from a Car-Window*, p. 85.

COLORADO

COLORADO: A SUMMER TRIP.

———◆———

I.

A GLIMPSE OF KANSAS.

LAWRENCE, KANSAS, *June* 8, 1866.

WHOEVER visits Kansas has the choice of two routes from St. Louis, — the North Missouri Railroad to St. Joseph, and the Pacific Railroad to Kansas City. The former is three hundred and five miles long, and the trains run at the rate of twelve and a half miles an hour; the latter has a length of two hundred and eighty-three miles, and a speed of fifteen miles an hour is attained. The former has the advantage of sleeping-cars ("palaces," I believe, is the western term — at least in advertisements), the latter of finer scenery. Having had a dismal experience of the former road some seven months ago, I chose the latter, and have been well repaid.

In the United States, railroads avoid the finest scenery, the best agricultural regions. This is especially the case in the West, where settlement followed the rivers and the old emigrant roads, forming belts of tolerably thorough cultivation, between which the country — even in Indiana and Ohio — is still comparatively rude. It is only within a few years that railroads have begun to *lead*, instead of follow settlement, and the line may soon be drawn beyond which they will represent the most rapid growth and the best cultivation.

1

This reflection was suggested to me while observing the country opened to the traveller's view by the Pacific Railroad, between St. Louis and Jefferson City. There are but three points which are at all picturesque, — the wooded and rocky banks of the sparkling Meramec, and the mouths of the beautiful Gasconade and Osage Rivers, — and none which exhibit much more than the primitive stage of agriculture. Yet the upland region, a few miles south of the line of the road, is, I am told, rich, well-farmed, and lovely to look upon.

Even when one reaches the Missouri, there is little in that ugliest of all rivers to divert one's attention. A single picture of the swift tide of liquid yellow mud, with its dull green wall of cotton-wood trees beyond, is equivalent to a panorama of the whole stream. For the seventy or eighty miles during which we skirted it, the turbid surface was unrelieved by a sail, unbroken by the paddles of a single steamer. Deserted, monotonous, hideous, treacherous, with its forever-shifting sands and snags, it almost seems to repel settlement, even as it repels poetry and art.

I travelled as far as Jefferson City in worshipful society, — five handcuffed burglars, three of whom had been Morgan's guerrillas. One of them, in utter opposition to all theories of physiognomy, strongly resembled a noted reformer. As the other passengers, in referring to incidents of the war, always said " Rebels " instead of " Confederates," I inferred that their political condition was healthy. Emigration is still rapidly pouring into the State, and, as a young man from one of the way-stations said, — " If we were only all Black Republicans, we 'd soon have the first State in the West."

When the road leaves the river, it enters one of the loveliest regions in the United States. The surface is a rolling prairie, yet with a very different undulation from that of the rolling prairies of Wisconsin and Northern Illinois. The swells are longer, with deeper and broader hollows between, and the soil appears to be of uniform fertility. On either side the range of vision extends for eight or ten miles, over great fields of the greenest grass and grain, dotted here and there with orchards, and crossed by long, narrow belts of timber, which mark the courses of streams. The horizon is a waving purple line, never suddenly broken, but never monotonous, like that of the prairies east of the Mississippi. Hedges of Osage orange are frequent; the fields are clean and smooth as a piece of broadcloth; the houses comfortable, and there is nothing to be seen of that roughness and shabbiness which usually marks a newly settled country. I have seen nothing west of the Alleghanies so attractive as this region, until I left Leavenworth this morning.

In the neighborhood of Sedalia, four or five hundred farmers, mostly from Ohio, have settled within the past year. I hear but one opinion in regard to the country south of the railroad, extending from the Osage River to the Arkansas line. Climate, soil, water, and scenery are described in the most rapturous terms. One of my fellow-passengers, pointing to the beautiful landscapes gradually unrolling on either hand, said, — " This is nothing to it ! " Yet I was well satisfied with what I saw, and feasted my eyes on the green slopes and swells until they grew dark in the twilight.

On reaching Kansas City, the train runs directly to the levee, and the traveller is enabled to go directly on board the Leavenworth boat, thus escaping the necessity of stopping at the hotel. I was very grateful for this fact, and having already seen the forty miles of cotton-wood and yellow mud between the two places, took my state-room with an immense sensation of relief. We reached Leavenworth at nine o'clock, in three days and ten hours from Philadelphia.

This is the liveliest and most thriving place west of the Mississippi River. The overland trade has built it up with

astonishing rapidity, and it now claims to have a population
of 25,000.   Kansas City, its fierce rival, having suffered
more than one blockade during the war, Leavenworth shot
into sudden prosperity ; but now that trade has returned to
its old channels, Kansas City expects to recover her lost
ground.   It is a subject of great interest to the people of
the two places, and many are the speculations and predictions which one hears from both sides.   As to the present
ascendancy of Leavenworth, however, there is no question.
The town has both wealth and enterprise, and its people
seem to me to be remarkably shrewd and far-seeing.   In the
course of three or four weeks the two places will be connected by a railroad which follows the west bank of the
Missouri.

The Union Pacific Railroad (Eastern Division) opened
its branch road to Lawrence in May, and trains now run
regularly upon it, connecting with the main line for Topeka
and — San Francisco.   One of my objects in visiting Colorado being to take a superficial view of both railroad
routes to the Rocky Mountains, I decided to go out by
way of Fort Riley and the Smoky Hill, and return along
the Platte to Omaha, in Nebraska.   My first acquaintance
with the Pacific Railroad, therefore, commenced in Leavenworth.   The train starts from a rough piece of ground
outside of the town, follows the bank of the Missouri for
six or eight miles, and then strikes inland through a lateral
valley.

Here commence my new experiences.   I have never before been west of the Missouri River.   Let me now see
what is this Kansas which for twelve years past has been
such a noted geographical name — which has inspired some
thousands of political speeches, some noble poems, and one
of the worst paintings that mortal eye ever beheld.   The
very repetition of a name, even in the best cause, sometimes becomes a little wearisome.   I frankly confess I have
so often been asked, " Why don't you visit Kansas ? " that

I lost almost all desire of visiting Kansas. Now, however, I am here, and will see what there is to be seen.

We gradually rose from a bottom of rather ragged-looking timber, and entered a broad, sweeping, undulating region of grass. Cattle were plenty, pasturing in large flocks, and there were occasional log-cabins, great fields of corn where the thrifty blades just showed themselves above a superb growth of weeds, and smaller patches of oats or wheat. Everybody complained of the incessant rains, and this accounted for the weedy condition of the fields. The soil appeared to be completely saturated, and the action of the hot sun upon it produced almost visible vegetable growth.

Here I first witnessed a phenomenon of which I had often heard, — the spontaneous production of forests from prairie land. Hundreds of acres, which the cultivated fields beyond had protected against the annual inundation of fire, were completely covered with young oak and hickory trees, from four to six feet in height. In twenty years more these thickets will be forests. Thus, two charges made against Kansas seemed to be disproved at once, — drought and want of timber, the former being exceptional, and the latter only a temporary circumstance.

The features of the landscape gradually assumed a certain regularity. The broad swells of soil narrowed into ridges, whose long, wavelike crests generally terminated in a short step, or parapet, of limestone rock, and then sloped down to the bottom-lands, at angles varying from 20° to 30°. Point came out behind point, on either side, evenly green to the summit, and showing with a wonderfully soft, sunny effect against the sky. Wherever a rill found its way between them, its course was marked by a line of timber. The counterpart of this region is not to be found in the United States ; yet there was a suggestion of other landscapes in it, which puzzled me considerably, until I happened to recall some parts of France, especially the valleys in the neighborhood of Epernay. Here, too, there was rather an air of old culture than of new settlement. Only the houses, gardens, and orchards were wanting.

As I leaned on the open windows of the car, enjoying the beautiful outlines of the hills, the pure, delicious breeze, and the bright colors of the wild-flowers, the bottom-lands over which we sped broadened into a plain, and the bluffs ran out to distant blue capes. Along their foot, apparently, the houses of a town showed through and above the timber, and on the top of the further hill a great windmill slowly turned its sails. This was Lawrence. How like a picture from Europe it seemed!

A kind resident met me at the station. We crossed the Kaw River (now almost as muddy as the Missouri), and drove up the main street, one hundred feet wide, where the first thing that is pointed out to every stranger is the single house left standing, when the town was laid in blood and ashes, in August, 1863. Lawrence has already completely arisen from her ruins, and suggests nothing of what she has endured. The great street, compactly built of brick, and swarming with traffic; the churches, the scattered private residences, embowered in gardens; the handsome college building on the hill, indicate long-continued prosperity, rather than the result of nearly ten years of warfare. The population of the town is now about 8000.

This afternoon my friends took me to Mount Oread (as I believe the bluff to the west is named), whence there is a lovely view of the Wakarusa Valley. Mexican *vaqueros* were guarding their horses on the grassy slopes, and down on the plain a Santa Fé train of wagons was encamped in a semicircle. Beyond the superb bottoms, checkered with fields and dotted with farm-houses, rose a line of undulating hills, with here and there an isolated, mound-like " butte," in the south. It was a picture of the purest pastoral beauty.

A little further there is a neglected cemetery where the

first martyrs of Kansas — Barbour among them — and the murdered of Lawrence lie buried. The stockades of the late war, and the intrenchments of the earlier and prophetic war, are, still to be seen upon the hill. So young a town, and such a history! Yet now all is peace, activity, and hopeful prosperity; and every one, looking upon the fair land around, can but pray that the end of its trial has been reached.

II.

JUNCTION CITY, KANSAS, THREE MILES WEST OF }
    FORT RILEY, *June* 20, 1866. }

As I recrossed the Kaw in order to take the train to Topeka, I felt that my stay in Lawrence had been too short.
The day was warm and cloudless, with a delightful prairie
breeze, and the softly tinted dells beyond the Wakarusa
invited excursions. The main street of the town began to
swarm with farmers' wagons, pouring in from the rich country to the south; the mechanics were at work upon new
buildings in all directions; the vans of the windmill on the
bluff were whirling merrily, and all sights and sounds spoke
of cheerful occupation. Fortunately, the people of Lawrence
do not expect their place to become "the greatest town in
the West, sir!" — so they are tolerably sure of a steady
and healthy growth for a good many years to come.

I reached Topeka—twenty-nine miles by rail—in an hour
and a half. The road is laid along the Kaw bottoms, on a
grade as nearly level as possible. The valley has an average breadth of five or six miles, and the uplands on the
north and south terminate in a succession of bluff headlands, which, with a general family likeness in their formation, present a constantly changing variety of outlines.
The lateral valleys repeat the features of the main valley,
on a smaller scale. Sometimes the bluffs retreat so as to
form a shelving semi-basin, or amphitheatre, a mile or two
deep, — a grand concave slope of uniform green, set against
the sky. At intervals of two or three miles the road crosses

tributary streams of the Kaw, flowing in narrow, sunken beds, the sides of which are fringed with trees. The landscapes have a breadth and harmonious beauty, such as I know not where else to find in the United States, outside of California.

Indeed, there is much in Kansas to remind one of California. These hills, now so green, must be a golden brown in the autumn; the black soil takes or loses moisture with equal rapidity; the air has the same keen, bracing flavor of life; and there seems to be some resemblance in the meteorological conditions of the two countries. Certainly, next to California, this is the most attractive State I have yet seen.

The grain-fields along the Kaw bottom were superb. I have seen no corn so forward, no wheat so close and heavy-headed, this year. The farmers were taking advantage of the day to work their corn-fields, the most of which were in sore need of the operation. Rank as is the wild grass of this region, the imported weeds have a still ranker growth. Last year's fields are completely hidden under crops of "horse-weed," every fence-corner has a grove of giant *datura* (Jamestown-weed), and the roads are lined with tall ranks of sunflowers. I saw no garden that was entirely clean, and, what struck me with more surprise, no attempt at an orchard. The beauty of the country lies in its natural features; cultivation, thus far, has not improved it.

Topeka, at present, is the end of passenger trains on the Pacific Railroad. In another week, however, they will run daily to Waumego, thirty-five miles further, or one hundred miles west of the Missouri River. We landed at a little cluster of shanties, newly sprung up among the sand and thickets on the north bank of the Kaw. Here an omnibus was in waiting, to convey us across the pontoon bridge — or rather two bridges, separated by a bushy island in the river. Beyond these the town commences, scattered over a gentle slope rising to the south for half a mile, when the land falls again toward a creek in the rear. I found comfortable quarters at the Capitol House. Mr. Greeley's "vanishing scale of civilization" has been pushed much further west since his overland trip in 1859.

Topeka is a pleasant town (city ?) of about 2500 inhabitants. The situation is perhaps not so striking as that of Lawrence, but it is very beautiful. Unfortunately, some parts of the place are destitute of water, which must now be hauled for the supply of families. There seemed to me to be a greater number of substantial private residences than in Lawrence. The building-stone — a buff-colored magnesian limestone, easily worked — appears to improve as we ascend the Kaw. It is found everywhere in the bluffs, and the handsomest buildings one sees are those constructed of it.

After calling upon Governor Crawford, and all the other State officers, — of whom I have to record that they are very amiable and pleasant gentlemen, — a friend treated me to a delightful drive into the adjacent country. Land, he informed me, is rapidly rising in value ; a farm adjoining the city on the east has just been sold for two hundred dollars per acre. The high price of grain for several years past, and the present rise in real estate, have been of great benefit to Kansas, enabling both farmers and speculators to extricate themselves from their former embarrassments.

It rained heavily during the night, and in the morning the roads were changed from dust to mud. Nevertheless, as I had arranged to take the overland coach at this place, thus saving myself twenty-four hours of fatiguing travel, I engaged a livery team for Manhattan, fifty-five miles west of Topeka. But I would advise any stranger visiting Kansas to make himself independent of livery-stables, if possible. The prices are rather more than double what they are in California. From Topeka to this place, my expenses for livery teams have averaged half a dollar per mile !

Leaving Topeka at nine o'clock, with some promise of better weather, we crossed to the north bank of the Kaw, and after floundering for a mile or two among mud-holes in the timber, emerged upon the open, grassy level of the valley. The sun came out bright and warm; the bluff capes and sweeping hills glittered in the light, fading from pure emerald into softest violet; tufts of crimson phlox, white larkspur, spikes of lilac campanulæ, and a golden-tinted *œnothera* flashed among the grass; and the lines and clumps of trees along the streams were as dark and rich as those of an English park. The landscapes were a continual feast to the eye, and each successive bend of the valley seemed to reveal a lovelier and more inspiring picture.

The larger streams we crossed — Soldier Creek and Cross Creek — did not issue from close ravines between the bluffs, as is usual in this formation, but each rejoiced in its broad rich belt of bottom-land, stretching away for miles to the northward. Most of these creeks are spanned by bridges, where a toll of from fifteen to twenty-five cents is charged. Their waters are clear and swift, and good mill-sites are already being selected. The advantages of the State, both in regard to wood and water, seem to me greater than has heretofore been represented.

After a drive of twenty-two miles, we reached a neat, whitewashed cabin, with the sign: "Hotel, A. P. Neddo." The landlord was a giant half-breed, remarkably handsome and remarkably heavy, familiarly known as "Big Aleck." He has four hundred acres of superb land, and is accounted wealthy. Big Aleck furnished us with a good dinner of ham, onions, radishes, and gooseberry-pie. Among the temporary guests was an Irish teamster, who had a great deal to say about Constantinople and the Sea of Azof.

Within four miles of Topeka commences the Pottawottamie Reservation, which extends westward along the Kaw for twenty or thirty miles. Many of the Indians are now

obtaining patents for their share of the land, in order to
sell to emigrants, and in a few years, doubtless, the entire
reservation will thus be disposed of. Here and there a
wretched cabin and a field of ill-cultivated corn denotes
the extent of Pottawottamie civilization. We met a number of Indians and squaws on horseback — one of the latter in a pink dress and wearing a round hat with upright
feather, and her hair in a net. A little further, we came
upon a mounted band of twenty or thirty, all drunk. My
driver showed a little uneasiness, but they drew aside to let
us pass, and a few hoots and howls were all the salutation
we received.

St. Mary's Mission is a village of a dozen houses, with a
Catholic chapel, on this reservation. My eyes were here
gladdened by the sight of a thriving peach orchard. The
house and garden of the priest, in their neatness and evidence of care, offer a good model to the Protestant farmers
in this part of Kansas, whose places, without exception,
have a slovenly and untidy aspect.

We had a drive of fourteen miles from the Mission to
the village of Louisville, on Rock Creek. The road swerved
away from the river, occasionally running over the low bluffs,
which gave me views of wonderful beauty both up and down
the Kaw Valley. Every mile or two we passed wagon or
mule trains, encamped near springs of water, their animals
luxuriating on the interminable harvest of grass. I was
amazed at the extent of the freight business across the
Plains; yet I am told that it has somewhat fallen off this
season. I have seen at least two thousand wagons between
Lawrence and this place.

The view of Rock Creek Valley, before we descended to
Louisville, was the finest I had had, up to that point. Even
my driver, an old resident of Kansas, broke into an exclamation of delight. The village, at the outlet of the valley,
had a tolerable future before it, until the railroad established the new town of Waumego, two and a half miles dis-

tant. In another week, the latter place will be the starting-point for the overland coaches, which will give it a temporary importance.

The bottom of Rock Creek is a bed of solid limestone, as smooth as a floor. Just above the crossing, a substantial dam has been built, which furnishes a good water-power. We did not stop here, but pushed on toward Manhattan, over the rolling hills to the north, whence we looked out upon grand distances, dark under the gathering clouds. By seven o'clock, the thunder drew nearer, and there was every indication of a violent storm. I therefore halted at Torrey's, a farm where the Overland coach changes horses, and was no sooner housed than the rain came down in torrents. The cabin furnished plain fare, and a tolerable bed, although the storm, which raged all night, leaked in many places through the roof.

Rising this morning at five o'clock, I found no abatement of the rain. We were soon sodden and mud-splashed from head to foot. The road, however, on the uplands, was beaten hard, and we made such good progress that we were at Manhattan, eight miles, in time for breakfast. This town, of five hundred inhabitants, is situated at the junction of the Big Blue with the Kaw. North of it rises the Blue Mound, a bluff three hundred feet in height, whence the view is said to be magnificent. There are five churches in the little place, and a mile in the rear, on a ridge, is the State Agricultural College, which already has one hundred and thirty pupils. The houses are mostly built of the beautiful magnesian limestone (resembling the Roman travertine), which gives the place a very neat and substantial air. This was all I could notice in the interval between breakfast and the harnessing of a new team for this place. With a Manhattan merchant as guide, I set out again in the dismal storm, slowly making headway through the quagmires of the bottom-lands.

I remarked that the bluffs were higher as we advanced,

the scenery more varied and picturesque, and, if possible, more beautiful. The wild-flowers grew in wonderful profusion and richness of color. I was surprised to see, at the foot of one of the bluffs, a splendid specimen of the *yucca filamentosa*, in flower. We crossed the Wild-Cat, a swift, clear stream, with magnificent timber on its bottoms, then Eureka Lake (a crooked slough dignified by that title), and after making ten very slow miles, reached Ogden, a German settlement, with a dozen houses, one brewery, and three beer-saloons. Here I saw one field of one hundred and twenty acres of superb corn, completely inclosed by a high stone wall.

More muddy bottom came, then low rolling hills, and in another hour we saw the buildings of Fort Riley, crowning a hill, two miles in advance. Before reaching the Fort, we passed the site of Pawnee, noted during Governor Reeder's administration, in the early days of Kansas. Except two stone houses, the town has entirely disappeared. The Fort is charmingly situated, the sweep of bluffs around it being seamed with picturesque, wooded ravines which descend to the Republican Fork. No wonder it is a favorite military station. I should have enjoyed it more but for the discouraging rain and the interminable mud.

We crossed the Republican on a floating bridge, and drove through three miles more of mud to this place, which occupies a rising ground at the base of the triangle formed by the Smoky Hill and the Republican Forks. It has four or five hundred inhabitants, a good hotel (the Eagle), and a handsome weekly newspaper, "The Junction City Union." Buildings — nearly all of stone — are going up rapidly, and trade is very brisk, in anticipation of the place soon being the temporary terminus of the Pacific Railroad. Passenger trains will reach Fort Riley by the first of August, and then a great part of the Overland business will no doubt be transacted here instead of at Leavenworth.

I must close, to catch the mail. The Denver coach has just come in. A through passenger, a fresh, rosy-cheeked boy, informs me that all is quiet along the route. To-morrow the coach I take will be here, and you will next hear of me from some station on "the Great American Desert."

III.

DENVER, COLORADO.

AFTER my arrival at Junction City, the rains which had flooded all Eastern Kansas, stopping stages and railroad trains alike, ceased entirely, and the weather became clear and fine. Although my main object in visiting Junction was to secure a good night's rest before setting out on the Plains, I was immediately requested to lecture that evening. There was no hall, the only one having been recently burned; no church yet completed; no announcement had been made — but in these far-western towns nothing is impossible. A store-building, just floored and plastered, without windows, and, indeed, occupied by carpenters at work, was selected; planks carried in for seats, a temporary platform built, messengers sent around to give private information to the people, and in two hours' time lo! there was a good audience assembled.

All Tuesday I waited vainly for the Overland stage-coach. The accounts from down the Kaw Valley represented the streams as being impassable, and toward sunset the enterprising population considered that my delay was now so far extended as to warrant a second lecture. With less time for preparation, they achieved the same result as the first night; and, truly, I have rarely had a more agreeable audience than the hundred persons who sat upon the planks in that unfinished store-building. What other people than the Americans would do such things?

While at Junction I witnessed a very interesting experi

ment.   The bluffs of magnesian limestone behind the town
precisely resemble, in color and texture, that which forms
the island of Malta.   In the quarry it has a pale buff tint,
with a soft, cheesy grain, which may be cut with a good
hatchet, or sawed with a common handsaw; yet, after
some exposure to the air, it becomes hard and assumes a
rich, warm color.   Messrs. McClure and Hopkins, of Junction, had just received a sawing-machine, driven by horse
power, and several rough blocks were awaiting the test.
Nothing could have been more satisfactory.   The saw cut
through the stone as easily and steadily as through a block
of wood, dressing a smooth face of eighteen inches square
in exactly two minutes.   The supply of stone being inexhaustible, this is the beginning of a business which may
make the future cities of Kansas and Missouri the most
beautiful in the world.

I stated the population of the place at four or five
hundred, but I am told it is nearly one thousand, each
building representing thrice the number of inhabitants as
in the East.   So I hasten to make the correction, for nothing annoys these frontier towns so much as either to under-
state their population or underestimate their prospective
importance.   Junction City will soon be the terminus of
railroad travel, and the starting-point of the great overland
freight business, which will give it certainly a temporary
importance.   The people, I find, desire that the road shall
run up the Republican Valley, in order to secure, at least,
the New-Mexican trade for a few years; but this is not a
matter to be decided by local interests or wishes.   The distance thence to Denver by the Republican route would be
one hundred and thirty-nine miles longer than by the
Smoky Hill route.

Another comfortable night at the Eagle Hotel, and
Wednesday came, warm and cloudless, without any sign of
the stage.   Mr. McClure kindly offered to drive me to Salina, the last settlement on the Smoky Hill Fork, forty-five

miles further, and we set out soon after breakfast. The road along the bottom being too deep, we took that leading over the rolling country to the north. Climbing through a little glen to the level of the bluffs, we had a charming backward view of the junction of the rivers, with the buildings of Fort Riley crowning the wooded slopes beyond; then forward, over many a rolling mile of the finest grazing land in the world. Two miles further we found a train of wagons just starting with supplies for the stage stations along the line. Mr. Stanton, the superintendent, informed me that he had come through from Denver to Fort Riley this spring, with ox-teams, in twenty-seven days. He expects to make three round trips this season, taking up corn, and bringing back lumber for the houses and stables to be built on the line.

We had occasional views over the bottoms of the Smoky Hill, which, the people claim, are even richer than those of the Kaw Valley; but that seems impossible. Twelve miles of pleasant travel brought us to Chapman's Creek, the first stage-station. Here, however, the stream was nine feet deep, and the people at the ranche informed us that we would have to take a ford two miles higher up. It seemed to me better to return to Junction and await the stage there, than to risk missing it by leaving the main road; so we put about and retraced our journey.

At noon, when we had reached the bluffs and were thinking of dinner, what should we see but the stage, at last, driving toward us from the town! Hunger, then, was to be my first experience on the Overland journey. We turned out of the road; I alighted with my baggage, and awaited the approach of a face well-known in the Tenth Street Studio Building. There were two passengers, but neither of them was my friend. In fact, the driver shouted to me before he pulled up his horses, " Your friend did n't come." One of the passengers handed me a letter from the agent at Topeka, informing me that Mr. Beard would probably not be able to reach that place for three or four days, on account of the floods. My arrangements in Denver would not allow me to wait; so I deposited myself, blankets and baggage, in the stage, and was fairly embarked for crossing the Plains.

I traversed, for the third time that day, the route to Chapman's Creek. The water was still rising, and we, therefore, tried the upper ford, and successfully. The road beyond this descended from the Smoky Hill, and followed the broad, level bottoms of that river. The soil was, indeed, of wonderful fertility, though but little of it, as yet, is under cultivation. Toward sunset we reached the village of Abilene, or Abeline (how or whence the name was derived I cannot imagine, unless it is an abbreviated corruption of "Abe Lincoln"), and here I determined on having something to eat. Upon questioning a stalwart fellow who hung upon the coach while it was crossing Mud Creek, he declared, with emphasis, " It's the last *square meal* you 'll get on the road!" My experience of a " square meal," therefore, is that it consists of strong black coffee, strips of pork fat fried to a sandy crispness, and half-baked, soggy, indigestible biscuits. For these I paid the square price of one dollar.

The sun set, — there was no moon, — and our coach made toilsome progress over the muddy bottoms toward the Solomon's Fork. Mosquitoes began their attacks, and thenceforth worried us the whole night. About ten o'clock the driver commenced an imitation of the bark of the coyote, which, it appeared, was a distant signal of our approach to the ferryman at the Solomon Crossing. It was too indistinct to note anything but the dark masses of timber on either side, and the gleam of water between; but from the length of time we occupied in crossing, I should judge that the stream is a hundred yards wide. The bottom-land along the Upper Solomon is said to be equal to any in Kansas, and emigration is fast pouring into it, as well as along the Republican and the Saline.

I should not wonder if " The Great American Desert " should finally be pronounced a myth. In my school geographies, it commenced at the western border of Missouri ; now, I believe, it is pushed some two hundred and fifty miles further west, leaving some of the finest agricultural land on the globe behind it. So far, I had found the reverse of a desert ; I determined, therefore, to be on the lookout, and duly note its present point of commencement.

What a weary drag we had that night over the deep mud between the Solomon and Saline Forks ! Either sleeping and stung to inflammation, or awake, weary, and smoking in desperate defence, two or three hours passed away, until the yelping and howling of the driver announced our approach to the Saline. In the dark, this river appeared to be nearly equal in volume to the Solomon. Its water is so salt as sometimes to affect the taste of the Smoky Hill at Junction City.

Nine miles more in the dark brought us to Salina, a village of two or three hundred inhabitants, and the end of settlement in this direction. Our driver kept us waiting two hours for a new bit for one of his bridles, and in this interval I snatched a little sleep. Of Salina I cannot say that I really saw anything, but I learned that it contains several stores and two physicians. The two or three houses near the tavern were shanties of frame or logs. Travellers west of Topeka are expected to sleep two in a bed, and several beds in a room. It was only through the courtesy of the landlord at Junction that I was exempted from this rule. In other respects customs are primitive, but not rough. People wash themselves more frequently than elsewhere (because it is more needed), and there is as much cleanliness in the cabins, all circumstances considered, as in many hotels which I have seen. I even noticed one man in Kansas, who carried a tooth-brush in his pocket, which he pulled out now and then to give his teeth a dry brushing.

On leaving Salina, the road strikes nearly due west across the rolling country, to cut off the great southern bend of the Smoky Hill. Two or three miles terminated the mud and mosquitoes ; we struck a dry, smooth road, a cool, delicious breeze, and great sweeps of green landscape, slowly brightening with the dawn. Distant bluffs and mounds broke the monotony of the horizon line, and the gradual, gentle undulations of the road were refreshing both to team and passengers.

By six o'clock we reached Pritchard's, the next station, sixteen miles from Salina. Here there was a stable of rough stones and mud, and a cabin cut out of the steep bank, with a rude roof of logs and mud. I was surprised by the sight of a pretty little girl of seven, and on entering the cabin found a woman engaged in getting our breakfast. The walls and floor were the bare soil ; there was a bed or two, a table, two short benches for seats, and a colony of tame prairie-dogs in one corner. I asked the little girl if she would not like a companion to play with, but she answered, — " I think I have more fun with the horses and prairie-dogs ! " What a western woman she will make !

Water was furnished plentifully for our ablutions, breakfast resembled the " square meal " of the preceding evening, with the addition of canned peaches, and we resumed our seats with a great sense of refreshment. The air of this region seems to take away all sense of fatigue ; it is cool and bracing, even at mid-day. Soon after starting, we saw a coyote sneaking along a meadow on our left ; then a huge gray wolf, at which one of my fellow-passengers fired without effect. He trotted away with a disdainful air, stopping now and then to look at us. At the same time a rattlesnake gave an angry signal by the roadside. There was no longer a question that we were now beyond civilization.

The limestone formation here gives place to a dark-red sandstone, which crops out of the ridges in rough, irregular walls and towers. Although rising to no great height, they nevertheless form picturesque and suggestive features of the landscape : in the distance they might frequently be taken for buildings.

The flora seems also to undergo a change. The grass was everywhere starred with large crimson anemones, a variety of the *helianthus*, with golden blossoms, a velvety flower of the richest brown and orange tints, white larkspurs, and dark-blue spiderwort. For many a league the country was one vast natural garden of splendid bloom. There were places where a single flower had usurped possession of a quarter-acre of soil, and made a dazzling bed of its own color. I have seen nothing like it, save on the hills of Palestine, in May.

After leaving Clear Creek, fourteen miles further, we approached the Smoky Hill. Two companies of the Second United States Cavalry were drawn up on the plain. Looking out, we beheld the encampment of Fort Ellsworth ahead of us. At present this is but a collection of temporary log barracks and stables, but the foundations of a permanent post have been laid on the rising ground, a little further from the river. We only stopped to deliver mails, but I had time for a brief interview with Lieutenant Lester, and a glass of excellent beer from a barrel in the sutler's quarters. General Palmer was inspecting the progress of the new fort, and I did not see him. Everybody — especially the private soldiers — was anxious to hear about the Fenian movement.

There had been no Indian troubles on the road, but the officers seemed to anticipate trouble from the continued absence of Indians from the country. The old trappers consider that withdrawal of intercourse, on the part of the Indians, indicates preparations for an attack. The Smoky Hill route, I find, is regarded with a little uneasiness this year, on account of the troubles last fall. The traders and train-men from Santa Fé represent that the tribes of the

Plains are not in an amiable mood; and I confess I am therefore surprised that a thoroughfare so important as the Smoky Hill route is not more efficiently guarded. As far as I can learn, the difficulty seems rather to lie in the existence of a mongrel band of outcasts from various tribes, half-breeds and a few whites, who are known, collectively, under the name of "Dog Indians." Most of the atrocities heretofore committed are charged upon this class, which ought to be extirpated at once.

When we reached the station at Buffalo Creek, ten miles from Fort Ellsworth, the driver surprised me by saying: "Here's where the attack happened, three weeks ago!" I had heard of no attack, and was informed by the agents of the line that none had occurred. The account the driver gave was, that a band of forty (Pawnees, he supposed) had stopped the coach, attempted to upset it, and made various insolent demonstrations for a while. One passenger, who made a show of resistance, was knocked down with a club. "There was a Commodore aboard," said the driver; "he was terribly scairt; and a woman, and *she* was the coolest of 'em all." This band is supposed to be under the command of Bent, a half-breed, son of the famous old frontiersman.

At the next station, Lost Creek (fifteen miles), we found a small detachment of soldiers posted. This looked threatening, but they assured us that everything was quiet. Thenceforth, indeed, we ceased to feel any anxiety; for, on a ridge, two miles away, we saw our first buffalo, — a dozen dark specks on the boundless green. Before night small herds of them grew quite frequent, making their appearance near us on both sides of the road. They set off on a slow, lumbering gallop at our approach, their humps tossing up and down behind each other, with the regular movement of small waves. Several shots were fired from the coach, but only one took effect, wounding a huge bull in the shoulder. It is this wanton killing of their game, simply in the way of amusement, which so exasperates the Indians. On the Smoky Hill bottoms, toward evening, we saw the largest herd, numbering some four or five hundred animals. The soldiers at Lost Creek had shot two or three the previous day. They had a quarter hanging upon the stake, but the meat both looked and smelled so disagreeably that I had no desire to taste it.

Antelopes and prairie-dogs also made their appearance in large numbers. The former were mostly single or in pairs, leaping nimbly along the elevations, or lifting their graceful heads in curiosity and watching us as we passed. The prairie-dogs sat upright at the doors of their underground habitations, and barked at us with a comical petulance. Toward evening their partners, the owls, came forth also to take the air. The rattlesnakes, I presume, were still in-doors, as we saw but two or three during the whole journey.

After passing a small stream near Fossil Creek, the driver suddenly stopped the team and jumped down from his seat. He leaned over the water, started back, took courage again, and presently held up to view a turtle which would weigh twenty-five or thirty pounds. The creature kicked and snapped viciously, as he was suspended by the tail, nor was his odor very attractive; but such a prospect for soup does not often arrive in this land of salt pork and indigestible biscuit; so he was tumbled into the boot, and the cover strapped down over him. For several miles, we on the back seat could hear him scratching behind us, but when the boot was opened at Big Creek Station, lo! no turtle was there. The driver's face was a picture of misery and disgust.

As the cool, grateful twilight came down upon the boundless swells of grass and flowers, I examined my sensations, and found that they were of pure, peaceful enjoyment in the new and beautiful world which I now beheld for the first time. The fatigue, so far, was trifling; the fear of

Indians had disappeared; the "square meals" had, some-how or other, managed to digest themselves; and I heartily congratulated myself on having undertaken the journey.

Here I leave you, one hundred and seventy-five miles west of Fort Riley, in the centre of what once was "The Great American Desert."

IV.

DENVER, C. T., *June* 18, 1866.

AT Fort Ellsworth I was informed that the military station between Fossil Creek and Big Creek had been dis-
continued; yet this is not the case. Toward sunset the
driver handed me a mail-bag, asking me to pick out the
letters for Fort Fletcher, the name given to this post; and
the assortment had scarcely been made, before the coach
was surrounded by a crowd of soldiers (apparently new re-
cruits) clamoring vociferously, first for tobacco and then
for newspapers. It was difficult to decide which want was
the keener. I gave them what cigars I had in my pocket,
but was destitute of papers, and could only inform them
that the Fenians had not yet taken Montreal. I felt no
less disappointed than the poor fellows themselves, that I
could not better supply their wants.

My companions were no less interested than myself in
the projected railroad routes to Colorado, and we therefore
scanned the Smoky Hill Valley from every elevation, with
regard to two considerations, — settlement and railroad ties.
So far, everything was favorable. The Smoky Hill was
everywhere marked by a line of timber, and we noticed
that at each junction with its numerous affluents, there were
large groves. The bluffs on the southern side were frequently covered, to their summits, with a growth of red
cedar. All the bottom-land is exceedingly rich and well
adapted for farming, while the broad, rolling uplands furnish the finest pasturage in the world. Near Big Creek,

coal has been found, and there are also rumors of tin and copper. With a sufficient force the road may be extended from Fort Riley to Big Creek in a year's time, and carry permanent settlement with it.

At Big Creek Station, which we reached after dark, we took on board Mr. Scott, the Superintendent of the Middle Division of the road. There was still no moon, and, fortunately, no mosquitoes also. The night was fresh, yet scarcely cool enough to require the blankets I had procured for the journey. Half-asleep and half-awake, now lulled into slumber by the slowness of our progress, now bumped into angry wakefulness in crossing some deep gully, we dragged through the night, and in the morning found ourselves at Downer's, forty-four miles further. Here an empty coach had just arrived from Denver, the third I had met going eastward without passengers. The Colorado people, it seems, are still afraid of this route.

Our breakfast here was another " square meal," — pork fat and half-baked biscuits. At all the stations the people complained of lack of supplies ; some were destitute of everything but beans. They gave us what they had, and we were very willing to pay a dollar rather than go hungry ; but one would naturally expect that where a stage goes decent food can be transported. As there is but one change of teams at the stations, we were obliged to take the same mules which had just arrived from Cornell Springs, twenty miles further ; hence our progress was very slow and discouraging. On arriving there, a second tired team was harnessed to carry us thirty miles, to Monument Station ; so that we lost full four hours during this day's journey.

The driver of the down coach informed us that the Cheyennes had appeared at Monument Station the day before, but they had committed no depredations, and appeared to be friendly. The chief had even invited him, on account of his red hair, to join their tribe. Mr. Scott, however, who has had eight years' experience of the Indians of the Plains, seemed to place little faith in their professions. They are reported to have declared that they must and will retain the Smoky Hill country, as it is the best range for game between the Missouri and the Rocky Mountains.

From the first rise after leaving Downer's, we saw, far away to the right, a long range of chalk bluffs, shining against a background of dark blue cloud. They seemed like a stretch of the southern coast of England, breasting the rolling green ocean of the Plains. Over great swells, covered with the short, sweet buffalo-grass, and starred with patches of crimson anemone, pink verbena, unknown orange and salmon-red flowers, we drove for two hours, watching the isolated towers and fantastic masses of rock detach themselves from the line of the bluff. They assumed the strangest and most unexpected forms. Here was a feudal castle of the Middle Ages; there a shattered, irregular obelisk, or broken pyramid; and finally, rising alone from the level of a meadow, we beheld three perpendicular towers, eighty feet high, resting on a common base. Their crests were of a bright orange hue, fading downward into white. Beyond them extended the shattered battlements of a city, sparkling in the sunshine. The blue ridges beyond the Smoky Hill, ten miles away, formed the background of this remarkable picture.

The green of the Plains here began to be varied with belts of dark purple, which we found to be what is called "bunch-grass," a very fine and wiry growth, but said to be excellent forage. At a distance it resembled the heather bloom on the English moors. Over these brilliant green and purple tints, the snowy fortresses of chalk started up with a dazzling effect. There is not the least approach to monotony in the scenery of the Plains; but continual, inspiring change.

We were to have another new experience that day. Our route, for some distance, lay over an elevated plateau, around which, for an hour or two, dark thunder-clouds collected. Out of one of these dropped a curtain of rain, gray in the centre, but of an intense indigo hue at the edges. It slowly passed us on the north, split, from one minute to another, by streaks of vivid rose-colored lightning, followed by deafening detonating peals ; when, just as we seemed to have escaped, it suddenly wheeled and burst upon us.

It was like a white squall on a tropic sea. We had not lowered the canvas curtains of the coach before a dam gave way over our heads, and a torrent of mingled wind, rain, hail, and thunder overwhelmed us. The driver turned his mules as far as possible away from the wind, and stopped ; the coach rocked and reeled as if about to overturn ; the hail smote like volleys of musketry, and in less than fifteen minutes the whole plain lay four inches under water. I have never witnessed anything even approaching the violence of this storm ; it was a marvel that the mules escaped with their lives. The bullets of hail were nearly as large as pigeons' eggs, and the lightning played around us like a succession of Bengal fires. We laid the rifles in the bottom of the coach, and for half an hour sat in silence, holding down the curtain, and expecting every moment to be overturned. Then the tornado suddenly took breath, commenced again twice or thrice, and ceased as unexpectedly as it came.

For a short time the road was a swift stream, and the tufts of buffalo-grass rose out of an inundated plain, but the water soon found its level, and our journey was not delayed, as we had cause to fear. Presently Mr. Scott descried a huge rattlesnake, and we stopped the coach and jumped out. The rattles were too wet to give any sound, and the snake endeavored to escape. A German frontiersman who was with us fired a revolver which stunned rather than wounded the reptile. Then, poising a knife, he threw it with such a secure aim that the snake's head was pinned to the earth.   Cutting off the rattles, which I appropriated, we did him no further injury.

The Monument Station is so called from a collection of quadrangular chalk towers, which rise directly from the plain.   At first sight, they resemble a deserted city, with huge bastioned walls ; but on a nearer approach they separate into detached masses, some of which suggest colossal sitting statues.   It is almost impossible to divest one's mind of the impression that these are the remains of human art.   The station-house is built of large blocks, cut out with a hatchet and cemented with raw clay.   Here we found stone-ware instead of pewter, although the viands were about as "square" as those at the preceding stations. The Indians had not again made their appearance.   They professed to have a camp four or five miles further down the Smoky Hill, and I was a little disappointed that, after so many rumors and warnings, I was likely to get over the Plains without seeing a single redskin.

During this day's journey we kept more away from the Smoky Hill, but we still saw, from time to time, its line of timber and cedared bluffs in the distance.   Near Monument Station we found it much diminished in volume, but with good, arable bottom-lands.   Up to this point, two hundred and fifty miles west of Fort Riley, we could not detect the least impediment to the construction of a railroad.   Nor was there yet any indication of the Great American Desert.

We had now shorter stations for some distance, and made the distance to Pond Creek, forty-six miles, by two o'clock in the morning.   It was scarcely possible to sleep, and yet we were too much fatigued to keep entirely awake. I have an indistinct impression that there was a two-story frame house at Pond Creek, and that we were delayed there for an hour or two.   I know that Mr. Scott informed us, as he took leave, that we were two hundred and twenty-five miles from Denver.   At this point there is a new military post, called Fort Wallace. Fort Lyon, on the Arkansas, is but forty-five miles distant, in a southwestern direction, and the road thence to Santa Fé about four hundred miles further. If the Eastern Branch of the Pacific Railroad should follow the Smoky Hill route (which is certainly the shortest and most practicable), Pond Creek will probably become, for a while, the starting-point of New Mexican travel and traffic.

We reached Willow Springs, eighteen miles, by sunrise. A forlorn place it was! The station-men lived in holes cut in a high clay bank, and their mules had similar half-subterranean lodgings. I saw no provisions, and they said they could give us no breakfast. The team was speedily changed, and we set out for Cheyenne Wells, twenty-five miles distant, through a country more nearly approaching barrenness than any we had yet seen. The timber almost entirely disappeared ; the lateral streams ceased, and finally the Smoky Hill itself, now so near its source, became a bed of waterless sand. Still there was buffalo-grass everywhere, and the antelopes were very abundant. The fresh, delicious air of the Plains — only equalled by that of the African Desert — refreshed us after the wearisome night, and our appetites became keen with enforced fasting.

At Cheyenne Wells we found a large and handsome frame stable for the mules, but no dwelling. The people lived in a natural cave, extending for some thirty feet under the bluff. But there was a woman, and when we saw her we augured good fortunes. Truly enough, under the roof of conglomerate limestone, in the cave's dim twilight, we sat down to antelope steak, tomatoes, bread, pickles, and potatoes — a royal meal, after two days of detestable fare.

Here we saw the last of Smoky Hill Fork. The road strikes across a broad plateau for twenty miles, and then descends to the Big Sandy, a branch of the Arkansas. It is a fine, hard, natural highway, over which we made good

time. The country swarmed with antelopes, which provoked several shots from the coach, but without effect.
Two of them, to our surprise, appeared to be pursuing a
large gray wolf. They made boldly after it as often as
it stopped, and were evidently bent on driving it quite
away from their pasturage. While we were speculating on
their movements, a lovely little fawn sprang up from the
grass and made away over the hills. The old antelopes
were evidently its parents, and their boldness in facing and
intimidating the wolf was now explained.

From the western edge of the water-shed, we overlooked
many a league of brown, monotonous, treeless country,
through which meandered, not the water, but the dry,
sandy bed of the Big Sandy. We really seemed to have
reached at last the Great American Desert. At the stage
station we found two men living in a hole in the ground,
with nothing but alkaline water to offer us. I tasted it,
and finding the flavor not disagreeable, drank — which
brought later woe upon me. Beyond this point even the
buffalo-grass died out, and we rolled along in the burning
sun and acrid dust, over dreary, gray undulations of weeds
and cactus. At Grady's Station, eighteen miles further,
there was but one man, a lonely troglodyte, burrowing in
the bank like a cliff-swallow.

Very soon, however, the grass began to appear again,
the country became green, and the signs of desolation van-
ished. A distance of forty miles embraced all we had
seen of the Desert — in fact, all there is of it upon this
route. In these forty miles a scattered settlement here
and there is not impossible, but is very unlikely. The adjoining country, for a hundred miles both to the east and
west, is adapted to grazing, and will support a moderate
population. The road, however, will soon be carried from
Cheyenne Wells up the divide, entirely avoiding the Big
Sandy. This new route, I am told, shortens the distance
to Denver by twenty miles, and has good grass and water
all the way.

Toward evening I was struck with a peculiar tint in the shadow of a cloud along the horizon. After half an hour's study, I pronounced it to be a mountain — and, of course, Pike's Peak. My fellow-travellers dissented at first from this opinion, but as the clouds dissolved, the outline of a snowy peak came out sharp and clear. It was something like that of the Jungfrau, but stood alone, surrounded by no sisterhood of Alps. At sunset we saw not only Pike's Peak, but the tops of the Sangre de Cristo range, and the Spanish Peaks, like little pimples on the line of the horizon.

What a night followed! The hard "hack" bumped and jolted over the rough roads; we were flung backward and forward, right and left, pummelled, pounded, and bruised, not only out of sleep, but out of temper, and into pain and exasperation. At one o'clock yesterday morning we were at Hedinger's Lake, ninety-seven miles from Denver. I thanked Heaven that no fifth night in the coach awaited me. The hours dragged on with incredible slowness, until dawn brought some refreshment, showing us a country of high hills, occasional pine groves, and far-flashing snowy mountains.

Before sunset we drove into Denver; but of the last day's ride to-morrow!

3

V.

THE ROCKY MOUNTAINS AND DENVER.

DENVER, C. T., *June* 19, 1866.

FROM Hedinger's Lake to Denver a new cut-off has recently been made, shortening the distance about twenty miles. Ours was the last coach which passed over the old road, the stations and stock being taken up behind us, and transferred across the country to their new positions. The road from Cheyenne Wells to Denver is thus abridged by forty miles, making the entire distance from Fort Riley to the latter place four hundred and sixty miles. When the stations are shortened to an average of ten or twelve miles, and the road as well stocked as it should be, the trip can easily be made in three days. By that time, the trains on the Pacific Railroad will be running to Fort Riley, and twenty-four hours more will bring the traveller to St. Louis.

I will not recapitulate our bruises during the night, but rather pass at once to the sparkling morning which broke upon us while crossing the divide between the Big Sandy and the first tributary of the Platte. In the foreground stretched a range of green, grassy hills, dotted with pasturing antelope, and crested with scattered groves of pine; high above and far beyond them towered the keen, shining wedges of the Rocky Mountains. Pike's Peak in the south was apparently near at hand, although seventy miles distant. Long's Peak, in the northwest, resembled an Alpine horn in its sharp, abrupt outline; and between these two furthest outposts of the snowy range arose many a nameless yet beautiful summit. The character of the scenery had completely changed since the preceding sunset. I was charmed out of all sense of fatigue, all feeling of discomfort, except that of hunger.

At Reed's Springs we obtained our last " square meal," with the inevitable bacon, for a dollar and a half. Thenceforth our road led over the high divides between the Beaver, Bijou, and Kiowa Creeks, all of which flow northward to the Platte. The country is grandly adapted to grazing, and all the bottom-lands are capable of being farmed. The pine along the ridges is of but moderate growth, but it will, no doubt, become better and more abundant with protection. A new flora here met us. The cactus, with its showy crimson and golden blossoms, became scarce. I found a splendid *euchroma*, with a spike of pure flame-color; great quantities of a wild vetch, with pink blossoms; and a thick growth of purple lupins. The grass was quite different from that on the plains, and many portions of these hills would furnish large quantities of wild hay. At some of the stations along the Smoky Hill, the men have mowing-machines, with which they harvest a full winter supply for their stock.

The view of the Rocky Mountains from the divide near Kiowa Creek is considered one of the finest in Colorado. From the breezy ridge, between scattered groups of pine, you look upon one hundred and fifty miles of the snowy range, from the Sangre de Cristo to the spurs away toward Laramie. In variety and harmony of form, in effect against the dark-blue sky, in breadth and grandeur, I know no *external* picture of the Alps which can be placed beside it. If you could take away the valley of the Rhone, and unite the Alps of Savoy with the Bernese Overland, you might obtain a tolerable idea of this view of the Rocky Mountains. Pike's Peak would then represent the Jungfrau; a nameless snowy giant in front of you, Monte Rosa; and Long's Peak, Mont Blanc. The altitudes very nearly correspond, and there is a certain similarity in the forms. The average height of the Rocky Mountains, however, surpasses that of the Alps.

Mid-day was intensely sultry, with the first dust we had experienced. We took a hasty dinner at Running Creek, and then made our slow way, with poor horses, across the ridges to Cherry Creek, which we struck about fifteen miles above Denver. Up to this point we had found no settlement, except two or three grazing ranches. The ride down Cherry Creek, through sand and dust, on the banks of the muddy stream, was the most tiresome part of the overland journey. Mile after mile went slowly by, and still there was no sign of cultivation. At last, four miles from the town, we reached a neat little tavern, beside which grew some cotton-woods. Here there were two or three ranches in the process of establishment. The water from the wells was very sweet and cold.

Our next sign of life was the evidence of death, — the unfenced cemetery of Denver, on the top of the ridge. I looked out ahead, from time to time, but could see neither horse, tree, fence, or other sign of habitation. My fellow-passengers had been loud in their praises of the place, and I therefore said nothing. Suddenly I perceived, through the dust, a stately square Gothic tower, and rubbed my eyes with a sense of incredulity. It was really true ; there was the tower, built of brick, well-proportioned and picturesque. Dwellings and cottages rose over the dip of the ridge, on either side ; brick blocks began to appear, and presently we were rolling through gay, animated streets, down the vistas of which the snowy ranges in the west were shining fairly in the setting sun. The coach drew up at the Pacific Hotel, where I found a hearty welcome and good quarters, and in just four days and six hours from Fort Riley I sat down, not to a " square meal," but to an excellent supper.

The two days which have since elapsed have given me a good superficial acquaintance with the place. First, let me say that the views which have appeared in the illustrated papers are simply caricatures. Instead of being a cluster of houses on a flat plain, with a range of clumsy mountains in the distance, and Pike's Peak standing alone in the centre thereof, it is built upon a gradual slope, rising eastward from the junction of Cherry Creek with the Platte. It is as well built as any town of equal size in the Mississippi Valley. The Methodist Church and Seminary, the banks and principal business houses, solidly constructed of brick (the former edifice with considerable architectural beauty), give the place an air of permanence, very surprising to one who has just arrived from the East. Beyond the Platte the land rises with a gentle, gradual slope, to the base of the Rocky Mountains, twelve miles distant, and there is no part of the town which does not afford a view of the great range. Long's Peak, more than 15,000 feet in height, just fills the vista of the principal business street. Pike's Peak is far to the left, overlooking the head of the Cherry Creek Valley ; consequently, a view of Denver, in which it is made the prominent feature, does not correctly represent the place.

Although business of all kinds is extraordinarily dull at present, and the people are therefore as much dispirited as Colorado nature will admit, Denver seems to me to have a very brisk and lively air. A number of substantial buildings are going up, there is constant movement in the streets, the hotels are crowded, and the people one meets are brimful of cheerful energy. The stores and warehouses are thoroughly stocked, and prices are lower than one would expect, considering the tedious and expensive land transportation. At the Pacific Hotel you pay four dollars per day, — no more than in New York, and have an equally good table. There may not be such an excessive bill of fare, but I could distinguish no difference in the cooking. Vegetables in the market are plenty and cheap, and appear to be of remarkably fine quality.

The dryness of the climate and occasional extremes of cold in winter, appear to me to be the principal drawbacks. Near the mouth of Cherry Creek there is a grove of venerable cotton-woods, and perhaps a dozen other specimens are dispersed singly through the lower part of the town. Attempts are now being made to colonize this tree — which makes a green spot, ugly though it be — around the houses in the higher streets, and with a fair prospect of success. The milk, cream, and butter from the adjoining farms are better than they are in most of the Western States. Venison and antelope are abundant, and canned fruits supply the want of fresh.

The situation of Denver is well selected. Were it nearer to the mountains, it would furnish a more convenient dépôt of supplies for the Clear Creek mining region, but it would not concentrate, as now, so many radiating lines of travel. It lies, apparently, in the centre of the chord of a shallow arc of the mountains, governing the entrances of some half-a-dozen different cañons, and overlooking a belt of farming land, fifty miles by ten in dimensions.

Its prosperity, of course, depends on the activity of mining operations in the mountains. There is at present a stagnation, occasioned principally by the enormous price of labor. Although the new methods of reduction promise a much greater production of the precious metals, and fresh discoveries of gold, silver, copper, and lead are being made every day, wages are so high that many companies have been forced to suspend business until the agricultural supplies at home, and the gradual approach of the Pacific Railroad, shall have brought prices down.

I should estimate the population of Denver at about six thousand. Probably no town in the country ever grew up under such discouraging circumstances, or has made more solid progress in the same length of time. It was once swept away by the inundation of Cherry Creek ; once or twice burned ; threatened with Secession ; cut off from intercourse with the East by Indian outbreaks; deprived of a great portion of its anticipated trade by our war; made to pay outrageously for its materials and supplies — and all this within seven years!

I was interested in noticing how attached the inhabitants are to the place. Nearly every one who had recently been East seemed rejoiced to return. Even ladies forget the greater luxuries and refinements of the Atlantic coast, when they see the Rocky Mountains once more. The people look upon this glorious Alpine view as one of the properties of the town. Every street opens (in one direction, at least) upon it; and the evening drives along the Platte or over the flowering ridges, become as beautiful as anÿ in the world, when the long line of snowy peaks flash down a brighter gold than ever was unpacked from their veins.

There are no manufactories as yet, except a brick-yard and two flour-mills — the latter driven by water-power. A good gray building stone is found about four miles off. The timber is all brought from the mountains, which, I fear, are in a fair way to become disforested. Coal, however, is coming into general use as fuel, several mines having already been opened in the neighborhood. It resembles the brown coal of Germany, burns freely, and is said to produce a great amount of gas. General Pierce, the Surveyor-General, considers the coal-bed of the Rocky Mountains one of the largest in the world. Along the Smoky Hill there are indications of an uninterrupted supply all the way to Kansas.

I find myself constantly returning to the point which my eyes seek, with unwearied interest, whenever I lift them from the paper. Ever since my arrival I have been studying the mountains. Their beauty and grandeur grow upon me with every hour of my stay. None of the illustrations accompanying the reports of exploration, and other Government documents, give any distinct idea of their variety and harmony of forms. Nowhere distorted or grotesque in outline, never monotonous, lovely in color and atmospheric effect, I may recall some mountain chains which equal, but none which surpass them. From this point there appears to be three tolerably distinct ranges. The first rises from two to three thousand feet above the level of the Plains ; it is cloven asunder by the cañons of the streams, streaked with dark lines of pine, which feather its summits, and sunny with steep slopes of pasture. Some distance behind it appears a second range of nearly double the height, more irregular in its masses, and of a dark, velvety, violet hue. Beyond, leaning against the sky, are the snowy peaks, nearly all of which are from thirteen to fifteen thousand feet above the sea. These three chains, with their varying but never discordant undulations, are as inspiring to the imagination as they are enchanting to the eye. They hint of concealed grandeurs in all the glens and parks among them, and yet hold you back with a doubt whether they can be more beautiful near at hand than when beheld at this distance.

To-morrow I shall move nearer their bases.

VI.

FARMING IN COLORADO.

GOLDEN CITY, C. T., *June 21, 1866.*

I VERILY think that if those who six years ago saw nothing but arid hills and fields of cactus, forbidding cultivation, could behold some parts of Colorado at present, they would open their eyes in astonishment. My approach to Denver did not furnish the least suggestion of farming, and all the attempts which one sees from the city are a few patches of vegetables along the Platte. But the agricultural interest, without which a mining community so remote as this cannot subsist, has really reached a development which is remarkable, when we consider the discouragements to which it has been subjected.

I am fast inclining toward the opinion that there is *no* American Desert on this side of the Rocky Mountains. Belts of arid and sandy soil there certainly are, but I doubt if any of these are more than fifty miles in breadth, while there are many points where an unbroken line of habitable territory may be followed from the Missouri to the base of the mountains. I remember that as late as 1859, the lowest computation of the extent of the Desert was two hundred miles; yet in the Smoky Hill route I saw less than fifty miles to which the term could properly be applied. What I have since learned of farming under these new conditions of climate and soil, leads me to suspect that time and settlement may subdue even this narrow belt; that there may some day be groves and farms on the treeless plains; that wheat may usurp the place of buffalo-grass, and potatoes drive out the cactus.

It almost seems as if Nature were in the habit of making a last desperate attempt to resist the subjugation of her wild, unploughed domains. For a few years the settlers are obliged to battle with a combination of hostile influences. The droughts of Kansas, and the grasshoppers of Utah and Colorado are exceptional agents, which have given a false impression in other parts of the Union. I found Kansas, as you may have noted, a land of rain, of soggy meadows, and swollen streams ; I find Colorado, where farming was pronounced almost hopeless, already crossed by zones of the richest agricultural promise. The effect of energy and industry upon the soil even now shows its fruits ; the effect of cultivation upon climate (an agency generally under-estimated) is yet to follow.

Two days ago Captain Sopris took me out to his farm on Clear Creek, about five miles from Denver. Crossing the new and substantial plank bridge over the Platte, we first glanced at the adjoining vegetable garden. I must con-fess, however, that I saw more sunflowers than anything else. Only a part of the garden appeared to be cultivated ; the soil was black and deep, and with proper care there would be but little limit to its productiveness. The profu-sion of sunflowers — not an indigenous growth, I believe — is remarkable. From Fort Riley to the Rocky Mountains, wherever a wagon has made a rut in the soil, there springs up a rank hedge of the plant. The pig-weed, horse-weed, and *datura stramonium* are also rapidly advancing westward. I found them some distance this side of Fort Ellsworth.

Rising to what are called "the second bottoms," a gently inclined shelf, extending from the mountains to the Platte, we had a view down the river, and saw the first in-dications of farming. Near at hand was a farm of three hundred and twenty acres, the owner of which is inclosing the whole with a high post-fence, at a cost of about two dollars and a half per rod. A neat cottage farm-house, at the commencement of the river-bottoms, pleasantly hinted of permanent occupation. Beyond this farm, still mostly in the rough, stretched a succession of dark-green fields of wheat, on both sides of the stream, which, divided into many arms, sparkled between its islands and banks of cotton-wood. The rising grounds were already beginning to grow tawny under the summer sun, and these low-lying belts of grain and trees made a dazzling contrast of color. For some miles down the Platte I could trace a continuous line of farms and preëmption cabins.

The undulating higher ground across which we struck in a straight line, toward Clear Creek, was covered with grass, lupins, a multitude of brilliant flowering-plants, and cactus. Dry as it appears, it furnishes good pasturage during the whole year, and irrigation will convert the whole of it into grain-fields. I remember that my admiration of the agricultural capacities of California, in 1849, subjected me to many derogatory epithets; hence, one who crosses these brown plains at the end of summer, may laugh incredulously when I say that all the country between the river and the mountains — every upland and ridge where water can be made to flow — will in time be as rich a farming region as any in the East. The capacity of soil to hold moisture will increase; trees will then grow where it would now be hopeless to plant them; hedges will take the place of costly fences, and the character of the country will undergo a complete change.

Captain Sopris's ranche is on a bluff overlooking the valley of Clear Creek. From the window of his parlor I looked out upon several miles of beautiful wheat, a long pasture-ridge beyond, and the grand summit of Long's Peak in the distance. Ten farmers here have united their forces, and made a ditch ten miles in length, by which their fields are irrigated. The usual yield of wheat, under this system, is thirty bushels to the acre, and the price, up to this time, has ranged from five to twenty-five cents per pound. You can see that farming, even at the lowest rates, is a good

business in Colorado   Oats produce about forty, and corn
fifty bushels to the acre, — the price ranging from two to five
dollars per bushel.

It is remarkable how soon the farmers have adapted
themselves to the new conditions of their occupation. They
seem already to prefer the secure yield which irrigation
offers, to the uncertain prospects of a more variable climate.   The principal labor and expense is the construction
of the irrigating canal ; that once made, it is an easy matter to watch and flood their fields whenever necessary.
This season it has not yet been generally needed ; but
from now until the end of July, when the wheat ripens,
the process must be frequently repeated.   Against the
plague of grasshoppers there is no protection ; this year,
however, promises to be free from that scourge.

The vegetables in the garden at the foot of the bluff
were thriving finely.   But out of three hundred grape-vines
which Captain S. has imported, only a dozen are now living.   Although the winters are remarkably mild, there are
now and then days of such extreme cold that vines and
fruit-trees of all kinds perish.   If the young trees were procured from Minnesota rather than nurseries further south,
they would probably be more likely to endure the climate.
Thus far the attempts at fruit-growing have been failures ;
yet the fact that at Salt Lake, much further to the north,
there has been perfect success, should encourage the Colorado farmers to try again.

After dining with the Captain and his amiable family,
we returned by a road skirting Clear Creek to Fisher's
Ranche, where I saw six hundred acres of grain in one
body.   The entire number of acres planted in the Territory
this year is estimated at seventy thousand — which will
supply the wants of the entire population.   The more sanguine expect to send a small surplus to Montana.   This is
really an astonishing fact.   In a Territory only seven years
old, six hundred miles from other settlements, which attracts

principally a mining and speculating population, and was supposed to have the most limited capacity for agriculture, the people are already independent, self-sustaining, in regard to food !

My friend, Mr. D. T. Smith, piloted me around the immediate neighborhood of Denver, and gave me further opportunities for strengthening the views which my trip to Clear Creek had suggested. I saw that the country to the east of Cherry Creek and the Platte is quite as fertile as that to the westward, and could easily credit the assertion of General Pierce that the supply of water is sufficient, with an adequate irrigating canal, to bring under cultivation four hundred thousand acres of land. I have no doubt it will be found true of all parts of the Plains, that wherever water can be had, farming will be profitable. Even where there are no running streams, wells with water-wheels driven by wind, as in California, may supply their place. An old frontiersman assured me that wherever there is a town of prairie-dogs, water will be found at a depth of from twenty to thirty feet. Now, in my memory, the road from Fort Ellsworth to the Platte is one grand prairie-dog metropolis ; so there ought to be no scarcity of water. In Kansas, living springs are making their appearance, as the country becomes cultivated. Nature, after vainly attempting to drive off Man, makes up her mind to reward his persistence. Perhaps I dwell a little pertinaciously upon this one point ; but, the truth is, I have never been more astonished than on finding this vast central region so very different from what previous accounts had led me to imagine.

A private company is now at work, constructing a large ditch, which is to water the streets and gardens of Denver. This will give the place the one charm it now lacks. Add verdure to its superb situation, and it will be one of the most delightful inland cities in the country. There is at present a small stream, the water of which is chiefly applied to the encouragement of young cotton-woods, both poplar and willow-leaved, which are set out so thickly around some houses that the owners evidently do not expect the half of them to grow. Some of the trees were flourishing vigorously, with a good prospect of life ; others, although irrigated, were withered and dying. The difference, no doubt, lay in the care with which they had been transplanted.

This morning I left Denver for my mountain tour. As far as this place, at the base of the first range, — a distance of about fifteen miles, — the country is rapidly coming under cultivation. Ditches are being carried from Clear Creek over all parts of the undulating slope stretching down from the mountains, and it was a cheering sight to find a large field of the greenest wheat upon one of the highest points, in the midst of a plain studded with cactus. A short distance from Denver, one of the ditches has been turned into a natural basin a mile in diameter, forming a lake of that extent, around which large herds of cattle were grazing. We found a number of men at work, constructing new ditches by a very simple process. Several furrows are first ploughed, and then the dirt is shovelled out rapidly by a broad frame of timber, drawn by horses in a lateral direction. Our course was sometimes impeded by the number of these ditches, which are not yet bridged, especially in descending toward Clear Creek, which we struck three miles below the point where it issues from the mountains.

Here we were favored by an invitation to visit the farm of Mr. Miles, and try the flavor of Colorado strawberries. This gentleman, I learn, sold his last year's wheat crop at eighteen cents the pound (ten dollars and eighty cents per bushel), and is now selling his entire stock of strawberries at ninety-six dollars a bushel ! The severe winter two or three years ago destroyed almost his entire stock of plants, but the few he saved are now richly repaying him for the loss.

Mr. Miles was not at home, but his wife welcomed us to their neat cottage of concrete, which, with the barn, stables, and haystacks, already wore an air of old settlement. The garden, though still in the rough, was very luxuriant. The strawberries (Albany Seedlings) seemed to me of smaller size, but of finer flavor than in the East. With the golden cream which our friendly hostess furnished, we could not have asked for anything more delicious. Around the house the lupin, coreopsis, larkspur, and sweet-pea were growing wild.

I here noticed a new, and to me a surprising, result of cultivation. Part of the bottom-land was originally alkaline, the white streaks being still discernible; yet the crops growing upon it were, if anything, more luxuriant than elsewhere. Captain West, my companion to Golden City, informed me that upon his own ranche an alkaline patch, bare of vegetation, has now become the best part of his garden. The use of manure is said to neutralize the alkali in a very short space of time.

Before us rose the curious elevation known as the Table Mountain. As seen from Denver it resembles a slice of cheese lying on its side, and with a crack through the middle. Immediately behind it is the first range of the Rocky Mountains, and this apparent crack is the cañon through which Clear Creek makes its way. On approaching nearer, the straight, slanting summit breaks into a very irregular outline, with bold, rocky buttresses and deep indentations. The top, on both sides of the Creek, is a *mesa*, or tableland, which furnishes superb pasturage for cattle throughout the entire year. A small lake supplies the herds with water, and the grass, however parched in autumn or dry in winter, never seems to lose its fattening properties.

A drive of about two miles through the gorge between the two parts of Table Mountain, brought us to the beautiful little circular valley in which Golden City lies hidden. Just above the place is the present limit of farming. The cañon of Clear Creek is walled in by steep, forbidding mountains, but there is pasturage on all the heights. Each one of the Creeks which issue from the mountains to join the Platte, is attracting a farming population. On Bear Creek, to the south, and the branches of Boulder Creek, to the north, I hear there are already many fine farms.

If a new system of agriculture has been learned, and such results attained within six years, is it too much to assert that the farming interests of Colorado will keep pace with the development of her extraordinary mineral wealth, and that, no matter what amount of population may hereafter be attracted to her mountains, her plains are capable of feeding them?

VII.

ENTERING THE ROCKY MOUNTAINS.

CENTRAL CITY, *June 23, 1866.*

GOLDEN CITY enjoys the distinction of being the capital of Colorado Territory. That is, the Legislature regularly meets there, but adjourns to Denver before transacting any other business. The population is not more than three or four hundred, and the place has a quiet and rather forlorn appearance at present. It possesses, nevertheless, several substantial stores, a school-house, two flour-mills (Clear Creek furnishing excellent water-power), and a manufactory of fire-brick. From this time forward it will rise in importance.

The discovery of coal is of scarcely less consequence to this region than that of gold and silver. Along the eastern base of the range, brown coal of excellent quality has been found for a distance of three hundred miles, and the indications continue through Montana. I saw, forty miles east of Denver, among the Platte Hills, a bold out-crop of coal, projecting two or three feet above the earth. Further in the mountain, the Albertine, or oil-bearing coal, yielding one hundred and four gallons to the ton, has been discovered. The supply of fuel for the Pacific Railroad, and for all smelting and manufacturing purposes, is therefore assured for centuries to come.

I visited the veins of fire-clay and coal, which are found in conjunction, within half a mile of Golden City. The clay is found in large beds of a chocolate color and greasy texture. Two horizontal shafts have been opened into the

4

side of the hill, and the carts are loaded directly at their mouths. The clay is first burned, then ground, after which it is moulded and pressed into the requisite forms. Although the business is in its very commencement, enough has been done to assure its entire success. The proprietors have already commenced the manufacture of tiles for roofing, which, I suspect, will ere long come into general use.

The coal, commencing at the surface with a streak of "color" (as the miners say of gold), broadens so rapidly that at the depth of twenty-five feet I found a vertical stratum fourteen feet in breadth. If it continues to increase at the same rate for one hundred feet further, the immense supply may easily be imagined. This Rocky Mountain coal, I understand, is always found in vertical seams, while the bituminous coal along the Smoky Hill Fork is disposed in horizontal strata. The valley of the Platte, after leaving the rolling country at the base of the mountains, appears to lie between the two formations. The examination, however, is so superficial, that nothing very positive can yet be asserted. Coal is beginning to be found abundantly in Southern Kansas, and it is possible that the gaps between the beds already discovered may yet be filled up.

Standing on this great bed of coal and fire-clay, at Golden City, I looked eastward across the creek, and saw a ridge of limestone rock, and the indications of a quarry which has just been opened. My companions pointed out to me the location of beds of the finest iron ore, all within the radius of a mile. The iron is said to be of unusually fine quality. Mr. Loveland of this place has proposed to erect a rolling-mill, and manufacture rails for the Pacific Company, enabling them to commence the road eastward from the base of the mountains, to meet the branches starting from Omaha and Wyandotte. Considering that all the requisite heavy machinery must be freighted across from the Missouri River, this would seem, at first sight, to be a hazardous enterprise; but, on the other hand, the saving in the cost of transporting rails for the road would be so immense, that I cannot pronounce the plan unreasonable. It is quite certain that all the rails for the central division of the road must be manufactured here and in Nevada.

There will, in time, be a railroad from the mining regions on the upper waters of Clear Creek to Golden City; and many of the companies will then find it to their advantage to establish their smelting works at the latter place. Let no one be deceived by present indications. The quiet of Golden City will not endure much longer; and the day may not be far off when the smokes from its tall chimneys, rising up behind Table Mountain, will be seen at Denver. I only wish that the vulgar, snobbish custom of attaching " City " to every place of more than three houses, could be stopped. From Illinois to California it has become a general nuisance, telling only of swagger and want of taste, not of growth. Why not call it " Goldenport " (as it will become a sort of harbor to which the ores will be shipped), or any other simple name? In the Russian language two unnecessary accents usurp one seventh of the typography; and in Colorado, if one talks much about the mining towns, he must add one seventh to his speech in repeating the useless word " City."

The age of law and order has not yet arrived. The people pointed out to me a tree, to which some of them had hung a Mexican, last week, on account of an attempted assault upon two ladies of the place. The criminal was taken from the sheriff's hands and lynched; and the few remaining Mexican residents, who appear to have had no fellowship with him, are ordered to leave the place. Affairs of this kind make an unpleasant impression. The improvised code of a new settlement is no longer necessary here, and it seems to exist by virtue of a lingering taste for rude and violent justice.

I found simple but clean quarters, and an excellent table, at Cheney's Hotel; addressed a limited audience in the even-

ing, and took the coach for this place yesterday morning, at
ten o'clock. The new road, following Clear Creek cañon,
has been made impassable by floods; and the old road, some
miles further eastward, is now used. It pierces the first
range of the Rocky Mountains by the cañon of a small
stream, at the mouth whereof are four or five log-houses,
styled Gate *City!* The defile is very narrow, abrupt, and
with such sudden turns that for a space the road seems
every moment to come to a sudden termination. Huge
masses of dark red and purple rock topple on either side;
there is little timber to be seen, but a profusion of wild
gooseberries and currants, and a bush resembling the
broom. The bed of the brook is crowded with young cotton-woods and box-elders, in the shade of which new varieties of wild flowers grow luxuriantly. I hailed the Alpine
harebell as an old friend, and inhaled the delicious per-
fume blown from clumps of mountain roses. The wild
hop-vine was very abundant, spreading its arms over the
rock, in lieu of other supports.

After two or three miles the pass became broader and
straighter, and we could look up to the crest of the mountains. It was dismal to see how much of the pine forests,
with which the steeps were clothed, have been wantonly
or carelessly destroyed by fire. The rock now appeared to
be a kind of gneiss, gray, with pale orange oxydations,
which gave the scenery something of the character of the
Apennines. I did not find, as I expected, much vegetation.
The dry soil, the bare masses of rock, the dusty road, and
the hot, cloudless sky overhead, all suggested Southern
Europe, rather than Switzerland or our mountain regions
of the East.

We followed this cañon for some eight or ten miles, occasionally passing a saw-mill, or tavern-ranche, patronized
by the freighters. Then we reached Guy's Hill, where the
road crosses the divide, and we were requested by the
driver to climb to the summit on foot. It was but half a

mile of rather breathless walking in the thin air, and we stood upon a narrow crest, overlooking a deep, pine-clad valley in the heart of the mountains. The dark summits of the second range rose against the sky, and only one small snowy peak was visible. Here the forests, although neither large nor dense, were still untouched, and multitudes of silvery aspens were mingled with the pines.

The descent looked dangerously steep; but our driver, with locked wheels, went down on a trot, passing two ox-teams with wonderful skill: The valley we now entered was greener and fresher than the first, and with a tolerably level bottom, along which we bowled to the Michigan House, where dinner awaited us, — an excellent meal, at one dollar and fifty cents. The water was unsurpassed in coolness and agreeable flavor.

The road now gradually swerved to the left, rising to another divide, whence the splendors of the snowy range burst upon us. Broad wedges of rock and snow, soaring to a height of fourteen thousand feet, glittered in the clear sky, apparently close at hand, although they were still fifteen miles distant. Our own elevation above the sea could not have been less than eight thousand feet. The air was thin, but wonderfully cool, pure, and transparent. The only thing the scene lacked was fresh mountain turf, — a feature which I have not yet found.

We descended from this crest into a deep glen, the sides of which were better wooded. Here and there we passed a grazing-ranche or saw-mill, and the road was filled with heavy freight teams. Two miles of rapid descent, and we suddenly emerged upon the cañon of North Clear Creek. Here commenced, at once, the indications of mining. The precipitous sides of the cañon were freckled with the holes and dirt-piles of experimental shafts; the swift waters of the stream had the hue of " tailings ; " and presently the smoke from the smelting works of the Lyons Company began to cloud the pure mountain air.

Beyond this point, which is already thickly studded with houses, and is called Lyonsville, a sudden turn in the road discloses a view of Black Hawk, with its charming church perched above the town, on the extremity of the headland which separates Gregory Gulch from that of Clear Creek. We at once entered a busy, noisy, thickly populated region. The puff of steam, the dull thump of the stamp-mills, and all the other sounds of machinery at work, filled the air; the road became a continuous street, with its hotels, stores, livery stables, and crowded dwelling-houses.

Turning into Gregory Gulch, we slowly mounted through Black Hawk and Mountain City to this place; but all three places form in reality one continuous town, more than two miles long, and with over six thousand inhabitants. The houses are jammed into the narrow bed of the cañon, employing all sorts of fantastic expedients to find room and support themselves. Under them a filthy stream falls down the defile over a succession of dams. It is a wonderfully curious and original place, strongly resembling Guanajuato in its position and surroundings.

VIII.

CENTRAL CITY AND BLACK HAWK.

CENTRAL CITY, COLORADO, *June* 25, 1866.

THIS place and the adjoining towns of Black Hawk and Nevada are so buried in the wrinkles and crevices of what I have termed the second range of the Rocky Mountains, that I could not fully comprehend their position until last evening, when I went upon the point called Bates Hill, which divides Gregory Gulch from the valley of North Clear Creek. On that station, the maze of mountains and gulches gradually untangled, and the relation of the different mining localities to each other became clear. The South Clear comes down from the snowy range in a southeasterly direction; while Gregory Gulch, rising from it at a general angle of about twenty degrees, extends nearly due west for about three miles, gradually losing itself in minor gulches and ravines among the summits of the mountains.

Black Hawk commences a little below the intersection, and thrusts an arm up either gorge, like the letter Y, except that the left-hand arm has outgrown the other, and now forms a continuous line of building and business, up Gregory Gulch to Mountain City, which is a connecting link between Black Hawk and Central City. The latter place continues the line of compact settlement up the bottom of the gulch for a mile further, and almost forms a connection with Nevada City, which occupies the highest position, near the summit. Black Hawk is exactly eight thousand feet above the sea, and the upper part of Nevada is at least a thousand feet higher.

The view of the intersecting ravines (they can hardly be called valleys, and " gulch " is a mining term) and the steep, ponderous mountains which inclose them, has a certain largeness and breadth of effect, but is by no means picturesque. The timber has been wholly cut away, except upon some of the more distant steeps, where its dark green is streaked with ghastly marks of fire. The great, awkwardly rounded mountains are cut up and down by the lines of paying " lodes," and pitted all over by the holes and heaps of rocks made either by prospectors or to secure claims. Nature seems to be suffering from an attack of confluent small-pox. My experience in California taught me that gold-mining utterly ruins the appearance of a country, and therefore I am not surprised at what I see here. On the contrary, this hideous slashing, tearing, and turning upside down is the surest indication of mineral wealth.

Commencing at Black Hawk, — where the sole pleasant object is the Presbyterian Church, white, tasteful, and charmingly placed on the last step of Bates Hill, above the chimneys and mills in the uniting ravines, — we mount Gregory Gulch by a rough, winding, dusty road, lined with crowded wooden buildings: hotels, with pompous names and limited accommodations; drinking saloons, — " lager beer " being a frequent sign; bakeries, log and frame dwelling-houses, idle mills, piles of rusty and useless machinery tumbled by the wayside, and now and then a cottage in the calico style, with all sorts of brackets and carved drop-cornices. In the centre of the gulch rushes a stream of muddy water, sometimes dammed up to broaden the bed and obtain a little more foothold for houses. Beyond the large mill built by ex-General Fitz-John Porter for an unfortunate New York company, who paid a large sum to repeat the experience of the National Government, Black Hawk terminates; but the houses, mills, drinking saloons, and shops continue just the same, and in another half-mile you find yourself in Central City.

This place consists mainly of one street, on the right-hand side of the gulch; the houses on your left, as you ascend, resting on high posts or scaffolding, over the deep bed of the stream. Half-way up there is a single cross-street some three hundred feet in length, where the principal stores are jammed together in an incredibly small space. With one exception, the buildings are frame, dry as tinder at this season; and a fire, starting at the top of the town, with a wind blowing down the ravine, would wipe out the place in half an hour. The whole string of four *cities* has a curious, rickety, temporary air, with their buildings standing as if on one leg, their big signs and little accommodations, the irregular, wandering, uneven street, and the bald, scarred, and pitted mountains on either side. Everything is odd, grotesque, unusual; but no feature can be called attractive.

I took quarters at the St. Nicholas Hotel, of which I will only say that the board is five dollars per day. The unaccustomed thinness of the air caused me considerable inconvenience at first. I felt a painful giddiness for an hour or two, could scarcely walk twenty steps without halting to take breath, and have had bleeding at the nose for three mornings in succession. This is a common complaint with new-comers, and the old settlers can always recognize such by their bloody pocket-handkerchiefs. The days are hot and rather sultry, but the mornings and evenings are lovely in their freshness, clearness, and the delicious purity of the air. Two things are hardly to be surpassed, — water and sleep. The water is like crystal, icy cold, and so agreeable to the palate that I am tempted to drink it when not thirsty. It is said to contain a slight proportion of alkali, and a common phrase among the people attributes their irregularities to the " thin air and alkali water." The properties of the latter, however, are said to be anaphrodisiac, which is rather an advantage than otherwise, in a new country. As for sleep, I don't know when I have found it so easy to obtain, or so difficult to relinquish. When I awake in the morning the half-conscious sense that I have been asleep is so luxurious that I immediately sleep again, and each permitted nap is sweeter than the last. The people seem to be remarkably healthy. Incipient disease of the lungs is almost always healed in this high and dry atmosphere, while it is fatal to the more advanced stages. Rheumatism and the mountain-fever are the most usual ailments. There is, at the same time, less tendency to disease, and less recuperative power when a person is once attacked.

In this population of from six to eight thousand souls, one finds representatives of all parts of the United States and Europe. Men of culture and education are plenty, yet not always to be distinguished by their dress or appearance. Society is still agreeably free and unconventional. People are so crowded together, live in so primitive a fashion for the most part, and are, perhaps (many of them), so glad to escape from restraint, that they are more natural, and hence more interesting than in the older States. Owing to the latter cause, no doubt, it is sometimes difficult to recognize the staid New Englander in the sunburnt individual in sombrero and riding-boots, who smokes his pipe, carries his pocket-flask, and tells any amount of rollicking stories. He has simply cast off his assumed shell and is himself; and I must confess I like him all the better.

Last Saturday night, at Black Hawk, at the close of a lecture in the pretty church already mentioned, a gentleman came to me and said : " It was a long way from here where we last met." He had a familiar face, but I could not at once detach it from the tens of thousands in my memory. " Do you remember," he asked, " riding into Kautokeino, in Lapland, one cold winter night, in a reindeer sled ? " " It is impossible ! " I exclaimed, recognizing Herr Berger, the Norwegian merchant, who took me into his house in that Arctic solitude, after twenty hours of frozen travel among the wastes of snow! It was he himself, come all the way from Hammerfest, in latitude 71°, to be, first a soldier in the Union Army, and now a miner in Colorado! He visited me yesterday, and we had a long talk about old times and mutual friends inside of the Arctic Circle. In three years he had lost every characteristic of the hyperborean, except an intense longing for the perpetual daylight of the Arctic summer.

The day before, I was suddenly accosted by a fellow-voyager from China to New York, *via* St. Helena; who, after enduring the horrors of Southern prisons, has come here to recruit as a mountaineer.

Perhaps the "thin air and alkali water" may account for the rage for owning "claims" and "lodes," which seems to possess all classes of the community. Every man you meet has his pocket full of "specimens." When you are introduced to a stranger he produces a piece of "blossom rock," a "sulphuret," or a "chloride." The landlord of the hotel where you stop confidentially informs you that he owns 25,000 feet — "the richest lode in the country — assays $1300 to the cord, sir!" The clerk is the happy possessor of 10,000 feet; the porter (where there is any) has at least 5000; while the chambermaid boasts of her own "Susanna Lode" or "Bridget Lode." The baker has specimens beside his bread; the dispenser of lager beer looks important and mysterious; the druggist is apt to give you "chlorides" instead of aperients; and the lawyer, who takes his fees in "feet" (money being scarce), dreams of realizing millions after the Pacific Railroad reaches Denver.

I have disgusted several individuals by refusing to buy, but the jargon has already infected my speech, and, after hearing a man at the table ask, — "Is there a *pay-streak* in that bacon?" I found myself on the point of asking the waiter to put a little more sulphuret in my coffee. The same waiter afterward said to me: "Pie's played out, sir!" If I had then requested him to "corral the tailings," he would have brought me the fragments from the other plates.

The Colorado dialect, in other respects, is peculiar. A dwelling-house is invariably styled " shebang ; " and the word, in many cases, is very appropriate. The Spanish *corral* (always mispronounced *correll*) has become completely naturalized, and is used as a verb, meaning to catch or collect. A supply of any kind is an " outfit ; " a man does not shout, but " lets a yell out of him ; " and one who makes a blunder " cuts open a dog." I cannot recall, at this moment, half the peculiarities of the dialect, but I am learning them as fast as possible, in order to conform to the ways of the country.

Some friends took me over the hill to Quartz Gulch, the other day, in order to try some mountain-brewed ale. After the intense still heat of the air the beverage was very refreshing, and greatly superior in its quality to the lager beer of the mountains. The owner of the brewery lives in a neat log-cabin, the steps whereto are ores of gold and silver, and inside the rough walls an accomplished lady sat down to her piano and played for us some choice compositions.

There is also a theatre here, with performances every night. Mr. Waldron, of California, takes the leading tragic and melodramatic parts, while Mr. Langrish, the manager, is himself a very admirable comedian. A good deal of swearing is introduced into the farces, to please the miners. I went in one evening and found the house crowded. There is a daily paper here, and one in Black Hawk, both well supported, I believe — certainly very well printed. The editorial dialect, to meet the tastes of the people, is of an exceedingly free-and-easy character. A collection of very curious specimens, both of approbation and attack, might easily be made ; but I am too fatigued by the thin air to make the attempt to-night.

I must also postpone an account of mining operations and interests until to-morrow.

IX.

MINING AND MINING PROCESSES.

CENTRAL CITY, COLORADO, *June 26*, 1866.

ALTHOUGH I have come to Colorado to look at scenery rather than at gold and silver mines, it is impossible to remain in the centre of mining operations without feeling a desire to learn something concerning their character and prospects. Indeed it is quite necessary to acquire some general knowledge of the peculiarities of the ores and the technical terms describing them, in order both to understand three fourths of the conversation one hears, and to avoid the enthusiastic explanations which would be immediately proffered if one should confess entire ignorance. One would soon " cap out," or " peter out," socially, if he did not yield so much to this community.

The region hereabout first drew miners, and afterward capitalists, from the rich discoveries made by Gregory, in the spring of 1859, and from its greater proximity to Denver. It is but one of a long chain of gold-bearing districts, many of which are still but half explored. Many more, no doubt, are yet undiscovered. Here, however, the most has been done in the way of development, and we can therefore better judge what dependence can be placed on the promise of the precious minerals. The deserted mills, the idle wheels, and the empty shafts and drifts for miles along this and the adjoining ravines — the general decrease of population everywhere in the mountains — indicate a period of doubt and transition, which is now, I believe, on the point of passing away. Colorado has been, alternately, the scene of exorbitant hopes and equally extravagant disappointments. Out of these violent reactions a new order of things is gradually being evolved. Great mistakes have been made. Ignorance has learned (at an enormous expense) to recognize itself. A terrible deal of swindling has been perpetrated, and the natural result is, that the country now has a worse reputation than it deserves, in most parts of the Union. As I do not own, or propose to own, one foot of any lode in the Territory, my own opinions on the subject — whatever they may be worth — will be at least unprejudiced.

In the first place, gold is found here under very different conditions from those of California. " Free gold," as it is called (native or virgin gold), is much less abundant. Owing to the conformation of the mountains, there is but a limited space for " gulch " or surface washing, and the rush of miners to the country in 1859 and '60 soon exhausted the best of these. The " blossom-rock " (partially disintegrated quartz, with the gold mostly in a " free " state) gradually followed, leaving the great storehouse of the mountains still untouched, but containing the gold in such stubborn and difficult combinations, that by the old processes from fifty to eighty per cent. was lost, or, as they say here, " went down the creek." Then came discouragement, despondency, failure of experiments, and a general collapse, the results of which are everywhere apparent. Yet new lodes were all the time being discovered, and each succeeding assay showed the richness of the mineral.

As a general rule the gold is found in combination with copper, and the silver with lead. The silver ore, in fact, is simply a very rich argentiferous galena. Some mineralogists say that the ores are copper and lead, in reality, holding the nobler metals in combination. It is immaterial which name we give, provided the latter can be completely extracted by some cheap method. This is now the problem which is vexing Colorado — which suspends enterprise and holds back emigration, for a time. Out of the many processes proposed, two only have been put in operation — Keith's and Lyon's. Monnier's and Kenyon's have not yet been actively tested. A few of the old stamp-mills are still running, and those companies which can afford to mine their ores a considerable time in advance of crushing them, will still make a profit by this method. The yield of gold is said to be fully doubled, by allowing the ore to be exposed to the air for the space of a year. Probably two thirds of the companies, however, are waiting the result of experiments.

Another cause operates, though in a less degree, to check enterprises on a larger scale. Labor is scarce and very dear. Mechanics demand from six to ten dollars, and the commonest miner five dollars per day. Iron, lime, chemical materials, and even fuel, are also very expensive. Moreover, nothing is more certain than that when wheat is supplied at three cents per pound instead of ten (as it probably will be this fall), and when freight from the East is reduced from fifteen to six cents per pound, the expense of mining and separating the metals will be less than one half of what it now is. For this good time, which is not only coming, but is actually near at hand, the whole mountain population is waiting.

The descent into a mine is one of the inevitable things which a traveller must perform. It is a moist, unpleasant business, but no one can speak authoritatively of " capping out," " wall rock," " flukin's," &c., who has not been down and seen the articles from beginning to end. Mr. Hayes, the Superintendent of the " Gregory Consolidated," offered to pilot me to a depth of three hundred feet, which I considered would be as much as a strict sense of duty could exact. I have no subterranean tastes, and honestly confess that I would have been glad of any valid excuse to omit the descent. But there was none: so I repaired to the engine-house and business office, high up the steep hill-side, put on stiff brown boots, a clayey coat, and a bespattered slouch of a hat, received my tallow candle with a sigh, and inspected with a new interest the photograph of Speaker Colfax and his party, taken after their return from the realms under my feet.

The steam-engine was undergoing repairs, and two hundred and fifty feet of perpendicular ladders, beside the pump-shaft, furnished the only means of descent.   Mr. Rule, the never-tired Cornishman, led the way ; then Mr. Hayes, with his tallow candle, while I, with mine, brought up the rear.   Through a little trap-door we passed from the blazing noon sunshine into a square, upright box of damp darkness, filled, somewhere far below, with sounds of dropping and trickling water.   The ladders are about sixteen feet in length, separated by narrow platforms, where we can now and then take breath.   On one side is the well, with its iron tubes, vanishing above and below.   I cannot pretend to describe the operation of the machinery, and will only say that the work is of the most massive and durable character.   There was plenty of leisure to inspect it before we reached the bottom.

Having accomplished the descent, I found myself in a horizontal drift, which followed the direction of the lode, into the heart of the mountain.   Moving lights in the distance, and the sounds of pick and hammer, guided us to the further end, where the workmen were busy tunnelling into the stubborn rock — the design being to carry the drift to the limit of the Company's property.   A new drift, seventy-five feet below this, has been started, and will be carried, horizontally, to the same point ; after which, the crevice will be worked out from below upward.   Its width, at the depth I reached, is from four to six feet.   Contrary to the experience of other mining countries, the ore becomes richer as you descend, though at the same time more refractory.

The lodes, in this region, appear to be nearly vertical, and are so much alike in their features that a description of one will answer for all. The vertical crevice, sunk to an unknown depth in the primitive rock, has sides more or less curved or waved, so that one side, from irregular upheaval, sometimes overlaps the other: the granite, or gneiss, meets, and cuts off the streak of ore. This is called " capping out." The first discovery thereof occasioned a good deal of consternation. It was supposed that the lode was at an end, and that, in all probability, the Rocky Mountains were only rich on the surface. Now, however, when a lode caps out, the owner strikes through the isthmus of " wall rock," certain of finding his " pay streak" below. Sometimes the lode is only " pinched," not entirely cut off. Of course the crevices vary in width and the ores in richness, but there is great similarity in all other conditions.

It was easy to track the glittering presence of the sulphurets and pyrites along the walls of the drift. When a light was held near the rock, it brought out sparkles of golden, scarlet, pink, and bright blue lustre, equal to any peacock coal. This ore, which is accounted very rich, is found in large masses, and it required a vigorous handling of the pick to get off a few specimens. I found it difficult to obtain any clear estimates of the yield. The ore is absurdly measured by " cords," — an ordinary two-horse wagon-load being called a quarter of a cord — and one cord may represent from eight to twelve tons. Fifty dollars a ton may perhaps represent a fair average yield — but this is a guess rather than a calculation.

Crossing a gulf on a suspended ladder, we climbed into an upper drift, communicating with a part of the crevice which had been worked down from above, and gave us a distant glimpse of daylight. Here we found the lode again, and could make some estimate of the value of the ores packed between us and the bottom of the mine. The way in which the lodes are cut into claims, which fall into the

5

hands of different companies, is a great obstacle to the economical working of them.   A horizontal drift, from the point where the lode strikes the bottom of Gregory Gulch, would be a self-acting drain ; but the Company, since it does not own this portion of the lode, is driven to the enormous expense of pumping from a depth of nearly four hundred feet.   Moreover, when one company suspends operations for a time, and the water collects, the companies above it, on the same lode, are unable to work.   These are some of the inevitable, yet very unpractical, features which still belong to Colorado mining.

As we were returning to the lower drift, there was a sudden smothered bellowing under our feet, the granite heart of the mountain trembled, and our candles were extinguished in an instant.   It was not an agreeable sensation, especially when Mr. Rule informed me that another blast would follow the first.   However, the darkness and uncertainty soon came to an end.   We returned to the foot of the ladder, and, after a climb which, in that thin air, was a constant collapse to the lungs, we reached the daylight in a dripping, muddy, and tallow-spotted condition.

Mr. Hayes was kind enough to accompany me to the smelting-works of the Company, and point out the principal features of the Lyons process.   I shall not attempt to give a technical description.   The process, I believe, is imported from Wales, with very slight modifications.   The ores are ground, washed, released from the rock, desulphurized by heat, smelted, the gold and silver separated from the lead and copper, and finally delivered in cakes which contain about seventy-five per cent. *in weight*, of silver, and some eighty per cent. *in value*, of gold.   The lead and copper are not saved, except so much of the former as is used in smelting, in the form of litharge.

I believe this is the only process, at present, in operation, which saves the silver.   Whether the amount gained thereby is sufficient to balance the greater expense of reducing the ores, I cannot say. Professor Hill, who has just returned from Swansea, in company with Mr. Hermann, of the firm of Vivian & Co., brings a proposal, I am told, to send "mats" of the metals, unseparated, to Wales, the value of the copper alone being enough to pay the cost of transportation and smelting. Mr. Hermann considers the ores immensely rich, and has commenced a series of assays, the result of which, I presume, will not be immediately made public.

The only objection I have heard urged against the Lyons process is its expensive character. In other respects it must be satisfactory, since the Company is now buying the "tailings" of the stamp-mills, at the rate of fifty dollars per cord, for the purpose of smelting. Statements on either side must be received with a certain amount of allowance, and many communications are made to me which I forbear repeating. I can only say that the energy and activity displayed by the Lyons Company indicate success.

Mr. Lathrop took me to-day to Keith's Mill, which is in the Clear Creek Valley, about a mile from Black Hawk. The process here is very simple. The ore, after being ground, is placed in hollow cylinders, where a number of small iron balls reduce it to powder. After being desulphurized by heat, it is placed in the cylinders and pulverized a second time. Finally, the usual treatment, by water and quicksilver, is employed to take up the gold alone, silver, lead, and copper being lost. Mr. Keith claims that by the process he obtains one hundred per cent. more than the stamp-mills — probably eighty to eighty-five per cent. of the whole amount of gold. The advantage of his method is its cheapness. The handling of the material, from first to last, is done by machinery, and the different stages of the process are so conveniently connected that four men can reduce two cords of ore daily. Mr. Keith seems to have great faith in the success of his method, which is certainly destined to supersede the stamp-mills. The loss of the silver, however, strikes me as an objection to its use in many parts of Colorado.

The stamp-mill of the Black Hawk Company is still at work, pounding out the less refractory ores from the Bobtail Lode. It is a model mill of the kind, admirable in its arrangement, thoroughly regulated, and with a refreshing air of permanence in all its departments. I am told that its average production is two hundred and twenty-five ounces of gold per week, whereof twenty-five ounces are profit. I suspect this is only a guess.

One thing is certain: the mines of Colorado are among the richest in the world. I doubt whether either California or Nevada contains a greater amount of the precious metals than this section of the Rocky Mountains. These peaks, packed as they are with deep, rich veins — seamed and striped with the out-cropping of their hidden and reluctantly granted wealth — are not yet half explored. They are part of a grand deposit of treasure which will eventually be found to extend from Guanajuato and Real del Monte to the Mackenzie and Coppermine Rivers, and which, if properly worked, will yield a hundred millions a year for a thousand years! Colorado, alone, ought to furnish the amount of the national debt within the next century. *The gold is here,* and the silver, the copper, and lead, — possibly, platina (there are already rumors of it), — and all that is needed is invention, intelligence, and properly organized enterprise.

There is an immense number of fools in the world, and many of them either found their way to Colorado, or invested in mythical mines of fabulous productiveness. More than the usual amount of folly and swindling was located here for a time — hence the reaction, the effects of which are still felt.

Before leaving Central City, I must say that it is the most outrageously expensive place in Colorado. You pay more and get less for the money than in any other part of the world. I am already tired of these bald, clumsy shaped, pock-marked mountains ; this one long, windy, dusty street, with its perpetual menace of fire ; and this never-ending production of " specimens " and offer of " feet," and shall joyfully say good-by to-morrow morning.

X.

TO IDAHO AND EMPIRE.

My friends in Central City will not take offence when I say that I left — not them, but the place — with a cheerful sense of relief. I had been for four days jammed down among the torn and barren hills, and yearned mightily for a freer out-look and more attractive scenery. As the stage left the narrow ravine, through which the wind draws the dust as through a funnel, and climbed around the steep toward Russell's Gulch, the air seemed to become at once gentler and purer. The mountains, though still for the most part bare or gray, with burned forests, swept broadly into the distance ; and between their gaps, to the eastward, shimmered the hot blink of the Plains. There were specks of snow near their summits, but the dividing range to the west of us was still invisible.

Russell's Gulch, from top to bottom, — a distance, apparently, of two or three miles, — and all its branches, show the traces of gold-washing. The soil has been turned upside down, hollowed out and burrowed into, in every direction. Around the edges of this desolation stand the deserted cabins of the former miners, a chance one still occupied. I noticed, here and there, some feeble attempts at gulch mining, but the large new mill near the head of the glen was a better sign of enterprise. The stamp-mills, all of primitive pattern, were mostly idle ; yet every vein in this region is covered by claims, and the specimens they show are of great richness. Here, as elsewhere, the owners are waiting for the new process.

Our road led southward, across several shoulders or undulations of the range, gradually ascending, until we reached the divide between the waters of North and South Clear Creeks, at an elevation of more than nine thousand feet. Two or three peaks of dazzling snow came in sight, apparently very near us, so sharply were they relieved against the hard, dark blue of the sky. Segments of the Plains — scarcely to be distinguished from the sea — appeared to the eastward; while directly in front of us rose the three picturesque summits, which have been named the Chief, the Pappoose, and the Squaw. The first of these reaches a height of more than twelve thousand feet, its bare pyramidal summit shooting far above the timber line. It has several times been ascended.

The height from which one looks upon these mountains greatly lessens their apparent altitude, and thus diminishes the effect of the scenery. When you have penetrated so far within the Rocky Mountains that all view of the great Plains is shut out, you naturally measure the elevation of the ranges from the beds of the valleys. But these beds rise very rapidly as you advance, and you are constantly brought nearer the line where forests cease and snow begins. The thin air and deeper color of the sky indicate the level you have reached, but the mountains seem no higher than before.

After crossing the divide, the road descends to South Clear Creek, through a long, winding glen. I here noticed a bush-maple, a variety of the alder-tree, and great quantities of wild currants and gooseberries. Far and near, all over the steep sides and flanks of the mountains, were the traces of prospecters. In some places " blossom rock " had been found and abandoned, probably making a poor assay ; in others, holes had been quarried to the depth of six or eight feet without any perceptible result. In the narrowest part of the glen, however, we came upon a pile of fresh ore, which showed a strong " color," and was said to yield from two hundred to one thousand dollars per ton. One of the owners, at least, was very enthusiastic, and it was plainly to be seen that the vein was being actively worked.

While I was admiring the bold, grand outlines of the Chief, which became more and more striking as we descended, the glen suddenly opened, and we found ourselves in the valley of the South Clear. "Ah, this begins to be Alpine!" I exclaimed. Here, at last, there was a little breadth and space, — a floor from an eighth to a quarter of a mile in width, bordered by mountains, which towered up, up, behind their huge escarpments of rock, into the region of snow. Here the ranges were more detached, allowing something of form to be traced; the forests were not all burned or levelled; glimpses of green meadows shone down from the higher slopes; and the cold, clear stream, fed from the fields of melting snow, foamed and flashed in the sun.

We came at once upon a straggling village of log-huts, which, after having outlived a variety of names, is now called "Idaho," — the inhabitants fondly supposing that this word means "the gem of the mountains." [I need hardly say that the Indians have no such phrase. *Idaho* is believed to mean "rocks."] I here left the stage, Mr. Sisty having kindly offered to take me on to Empire in the afternoon. In this queer, almost aboriginal village, with its charming situation, there is the best hotel in Colorado. It has just been completed; the opening ball occurred after I reached Central City. The astonished stranger here finds a parlor with carpets as showy, horse-hair sofas as shiny and slippery, looking-glasses with as much gilding, tables as marbled-topped, and everything else as radiant with varnish or gypsum, as the laws of American taste in such things could require. The bedrooms are so fresh — so unsuggestive of a thousand unwashed previous occupants — that I regretted not being able to enjoy the luxury for one night.

While I was preparing to accompany Mr. Sisty to the soda springs of Idaho, I was accosted by an old Norwegian, a native of Drammen. The kindly feeling which all Scandinavians have for any one who has ever visited their country is remarkable. In Kansas, I bought a pair of blankets from a Swede, who instantly abated one dollar of the price, when I addressed him in his native tongue. Although my Norsk is very halting, from long disuse, the old fellow borrowed a fishing-rod, and in an hour presented me with seven mountain-trout for my dinner. And such trout! Admirable as was the hotel-dinner, over which Mrs. Beebe presided, I was obliged to slight it for the special dish she prepared and placed before me. I hope to fall in with many more Norwegians before I leave the mountains.

The soda springs are already turned to service. Two bath-houses have been built for summer guests. In one of these the water is so regulated, that the bather may choose whatever temperature he prefers, the hot spring being about ninety-five degrees as it issues from the earth. It has a deliciously refreshing and exhilarating quality, as I found after taking it warm. The taste resembles a weak and rather flat citrate of magnesia ; but, as the water has not yet been analyzed, I cannot give the ingredients. The hot and cold springs come up so close together, that one may dip a hand in either at the same time.

But neither these springs nor the gold mines comprise all the riches of Idaho. Further down the valley, somewhere, there is a vein of rough opal eighteen inches thick. I have a piece of it in my pocket at this moment, and it is undoubtedly opal, though of faint, imperfect fire, as if its quality were faded by long exposure to the weather. Small specimens of a similar variety, from Montana, are frequent in Colorado ; but I have seen nothing yet with the infinite sparkle of the Hungarian or the prismatic lustre of the Honduras opal. It is unreasonable, however, to ask for the precious gems, where so much other wealth has been given.

After dinner, Mr. Sisty produced a buggy and a pair of fast horses, and we set out up the valley. The road was smooth, as if macadamized ; the cold, pale-green creek roared beside us, sweeping around pine-clad capes or under the shadow of mighty cliffs, and the snows of the higher summits brightened in the sunshine. This was inspiring travel, reminding me (dimly, I must confess) of the Upper Valley of the Rhine, between Splügen and the Via Mala. After two or three miles the valley contracted, becoming a mere cañon, walled in by overhanging precipices ; a stream, which we crossed on a toll-bridge, came down through a gorge on the right. Beyond the bridge there was a hotel, commanding a view of the wonderful "Notch." I noticed that one of the upper windows of this hotel had been removed ; then I saw the end of a mahlstick moving about in the open place ; then a mass of flowing locks, an easel, and an absorbed countenance. It was Mr. Beard, working with might and main to catch the lovely, fleeting effects of light and shade on the rocks and pines. On the veranda below sat General Pierce, his companion, more patient than Science usually is, when it must wait for Art.

We halted an hour, and I made a wretched attempt at a sketch of the place. You cannot cram this scenery into the compass of a block-book; it requires a large canvas, and the boldest and broadest handling. The eye is continually cheated, the actual being so much more than the apparent dimensions of all objects. Though so familiar with the effect of extraordinarily pure, thin air, and great clearness of outline, I am still frequently at fault. What one *sees* small, is always small in the drawing. Even photographs here have the same dwarfed, diminished expression. I can now see how naturally Bierstadt was led to a large canvas.

Leaving the artist at his work, we drove through the gorge into another open stretch of the valley. Westward, directly in front, a peak of the central snowy range towered over all the intermediate heights; while on the left Mount Douglas, throwing its own shadow over a thousand feet of vertical precipice, guarded the entrance to Georgetown Valley. Three or four miles up this valley lies the little village of that name, with promising leads and lodes; while beyond it, among the snowy tangle of mountains at the southeastern corner of the Middle Park, is the famous silver district, recently discovered, and now known by the name of " Argentine." The mineral is there said to be of fabulous richness, but more than ten thousand feet above the sea. Assays, I am informed, give between three and four thousand dollars to the ton.

In ascending the South Clear, the rise averages about one hundred feet to the mile, and the estimated elevation of Empire is nine thousand feet. Take the altitude of the Catskill Mountain House above the Hudson, and place that on the top of Mount Washington, and you will have the elevation of this place, where people live, work, and carry on business; where, in the Rocky Mountains, cattle have excellent pasture, and potatoes are raised! More than this, the little mining village of North Empire, a mile from this place, is one thousand four hundred feet higher; yet even there the inhabitants pass the winter with less discomfort than one would suppose. On the table-lands of the Andes, under the equator, we find towns at an equal height, but nowhere else in the world. Among the Alps, at an elevation of nine thousand feet, there is not a blade of grass; even moss and lichens disappear.

Empire enjoys a very picturesque situation. The population may possibly be three hundred; the houses are mostly cabins of hewn logs, but their inhabitants are men of intelligence and enterprise. On reaching the White House (kept by Mr. White), I found Mr. Byers, editor of

" The Rocky Mountain News," who is to be our pilot and companion through the Parks. Mr. Beard has since arrived, and the other two gentlemen of our party (Messrs. M'Candless and Davis, of Pittsburg) were already awaiting us. Here, therefore, we shall take leave of such civilization as gold-mining carries with it, and strike into the wilder regions beyond. Our preparations are few and easily made. The horses and mules, belonging to Charley Utter, the famous trapper and trader of the Middle Park, will be in charge of Mr. White's son. Mr. Byers has superintended the laying in of supplies (consisting chiefly of biscuit, fat pork, ham, coffee, and sugar), and our blankets and overcoats will furnish the necessary bedding. Luxuries we discard — except, in my single case, a few cigars of doubtful quality. No cases of bottles, or boxes of tin cans, accompany us ; we have no forks, nor plates, but one tin cup apiece, and a single spoon for the whole company. The culinary utensils consist of a frying-pan and a coffee-pot. To be sure, we have visions of mountain-trout, and of elk-steak, broiled on skewers ; but these may be fairly permitted, without branding us as epicureans. The whole outfit is of the Robinson Crusoe character, and necessarily so, for pack animals must be lightly burdened on the trails which we are to follow.

—— I have just been lecturing in the Methodist church (the same in which the Colorado Conference has been held this week) to an audience of more than a hundred persons. The effect of speaking, at an altitude of nine thousand feet, is not attended with the fatigue which I had anticipated during the act ; but it is followed by a sense of complete exhaustion. The audience, for calm, steady attention, might have belonged to New York or New England. No one went out for a drink, as is the custom in the mining communities of California. I missed — and to my regret — a type of face which I have found in every Colorado audience, until this evening. In fact, I came to look for the face naturally; it struck my fancy in Denver, the first evening, and I found it, slightly varied, for eight nights in succession. It represents a type unique among civilized races, and only to be found (and that only of late years) in the United States — a type expressing the precise point where the elements of the rowdy begin to disappear, and those of the gentleman manifest themselves. The square of the face rounds into the oval; the forehead is good, the eyebrows straight and dark, the hair generally dark also; the eye is remarkably beautiful; the nose would be good, but for the least bit of tendency to turn up at the end; there is generally a mustache, full yet firm lips, a strong, manly chin, and (here the rowdy mark remains !) a square animal jaw. The face expresses a fine and noble quality of manhood, not yet wholly detached from a coarse, rude basis. This type so interested me, that I found myself involuntarily singling out the best specimen and addressing myself specially to him — and always with a sense that it was right to do so. I should be glad to think that this face represents a general fact.

XI.

CAMP IN THE MIDDLE PARK, *June* 29, 1866.

OUR plans for the mountain journey had been fixed before leaving Denver, and we adhered to them in spite of warnings and persuasions. Mr. Byers is an accomplished mountaineer, to whom much of the ground is familiar, and I preferred taking his advice to that of others who spoke from hearsay rather than experience. It would be difficult, if not impossible, to cross Berthoud Pass, many persons asserted; the hardships of Colonel Babcock's party, a fortnight ago, were constantly cited, and the spectres of risk and danger, which those who stay at home delight to evoke for those who travel, accompanied us up to the very moment of starting.

At Empire, however, the people contented themselves with predicting that we could not get over the Pass in a day; and, indeed, there seemed a strong probability that they were right. White set out at daybreak to corral the horses and mules; we also rose early, washed our faces in the frosty air, in the midst of a panorama of rose-tinted Alps, took an early "square" breakfast, and tied our equipments in comfortable parcels for packing. But the animals, well suspecting what was before them, refused to be corralled. First one assistant, then another, was dispatched, until five persons were busy, and nine o'clock had arrived before there was any prospect of our departure. In the mean time, the landlord produced a boiled ham, and a tin kettle full of hot biscuit, which we put into a coffee-bag.

"They might ha' been sadder," said he, speaking of the biscuit; "they pack better when they 're sad."

General Pierce had set out on his return to Denver, taking with him our "biled shirts and store clothes." We were attired in flannel, and becomingly rough, each with the handle of a tin cup hooked into the button-hole of his coat, his trousers tucked into huge riding-boots, spur on heel, and buckskin gloves on hand. By this time White had arrived with the animals, — two cute little pack-mules, a lean dun mare for myself, and a large brown mule for Mr. Beard. The other gentlemen had their own beasts. The packing, strapping, and other final preparations were done hastily, and by ten o'clock we were in the saddle. "You 'll camp on this side of the Pass to-night," said Judge Cowles; and so we rode out of Empire.

I wish we had a word in the English language corresponding to the German "*reiselust*" — because that word, and none other, expresses the feeling with which one sets out on a journey, in the pure upper air of a mountain region. The blood circulates with nimble alacrity; the lungs expand with a tingling sense of delight; all sights and sounds of Nature have a character of cheer and encouragement; life is a most agreeable condition, and one's fellow-men are good fellows, every one of them.

It was a superb day. The wind blew down from the snow-fields, tempering the heat of a dazzling sun in a cloudless sky. The village behind us showed between groups of tall, dark fir-trees; the creek, dammed for a stamp-mill, spread out a bright lake in the lap of the valley; and southward the sharp summit of Montgomery Peak rose high above all the surrounding mountains. We had still a good wagon-road, with rough bridges across the torrents which came down from every rocky glen. The pack-mules maliciously strayed hither and thither, shaking out of balance their hastily arranged loads, and sometimes even hiding behind the trees in the hope of escaping their destiny.

The valley gradually narrowed, and we entered a defile far grander than anything I had yet seen in the Rocky Mountains. On either side enormous masses of dark-red rock towered over our heads to the height of fifteen hundred feet, so torn and split into colossal towers, walls, and buttresses, that every minute presented a new combination of forms. The bed of the glen was filled with huge fragments, tumbled from above. Even here, high up on almost inaccessible points, the prospectors had left their traces, lured by the indications of ore in cliffs above, to which they dare not climb. Our necks ached with gazing at the sharp sky-piercing summits, in the hope of detecting mountain sheep; but none were to be seen.

We forded the South Clear, which, swollen by the melting snows, reached to the horses' bellies, and was so swift that they could scarcely keep their footing. The road then entered a forest of fir and pine, over the tops of which we now and then caught the glimmer of snowy summits. But the new and beautiful flora of the mountains kept my gaze to the earth. Both new flowers and new varieties of familiar families made their appearance. A lovely species of the columbine (*aquilegia*), large and white, the horns and external petals of a pale violet, would be a great ornament to our gardens. There were also several handsome varieties of sedum and saxifrage, the flame-colored euchroma, and an unknown spicy flower of the purest turquoise blue. The *mahonia*, here called the "Oregon grape," is very abundant in the forests. I have found it in all parts of the mountains which I have yet visited.

Beyond the rocky gorge which I have described, the valley opens again, revealing its head, inclosed by a semicircular sweep of the snowy range. As this is one of the points suggested for the passage of the Rocky Mountains by the Pacific Railroad, we took careful note of its conformation, and the facilities offered for overcoming the altitude of the range. The average fall of Clear Creek, from the base of the dividing ridge to the Plains near Denver, is about one hundred feet per mile, and there is no difficulty in building a road through that part of the valley which I traversed. On reaching the head of the valley, three passes offer themselves. The first is the famous Berthoud Pass, on the right, offering a way into the Middle Park through a depression in the main chain. Five miles further is the Vasquez Pass, also on the right hand. This, however, is rather a *trail*, over the crest of the mountain, than a *pass*. Some four or five miles further, at the very head of the valley, is a new pass, recently discovered by Mr. Jones, who is at present engaged in constructing a wagon-road over it into the Park. Both the latter passes are higher than the Berthoud, but the new one is said to offer the easiest approaches. It has not yet been surveyed, and may prove the most favorable for a railroad.

At the foot of the Berthoud Pass, we had already risen more than nine thousand feet above the sea, leaving about two thousand feet still to be surmounted. We were eight miles from Empire, and three from the summit. Our pack-mules were forced, with great difficulty, to leave the wagon-road, and take the narrow trail which struck directly up the steep flank of the mountain. It was, indeed, a terrible pull which awaited them. We had not made a hundred yards before our horses stopped, almost gasping for breath. I could feel the heart of my lean mare knocking rapidly against her ribs. A few little knobs or projections from the line of descent favored the poor beasts for awhile, but it was not long before these ceased, and the terrific slant of the mountain presented itself unrelieved, to be overcome. The trail was a mere mark in the gravelly soil, where a stone loosed by the foot would find no rest until it reached the level of the valley. The angle of descent was in some places not less than 50°. Here there were few trees, and the valley yawned under us like an enormous green basin, with a jagged white border.

6

From this point I overlooked the course of Clear Creek from its very source. The main valley seemed to be formed out of four or five small ones, radiating down from between the buttresses of the main chain. It appeared to be doubtful whether a railroad could obtain a sufficient return curve to overcome the first precipitous part of the Berthoud Pass without running up to the head of the valley on the opposite side — in which case, each of these lateral valleys, or rather glens, would be an obstacle. Still — judging merely by the eye — the difficulty did not seem to be much greater than in the case of the Pennsylvania Central, or the Baltimore and Ohio roads. What lay beyond the angle of the mountain we were climbing I could not see; but there is certainly valley enough above the foot of the Berthoud Pass to effect a rise of one thousand feet, which (with a tunnel three miles in length, cutting off fifteen hundred feet of elevation) is all that would be necessary.

Mr. Beard and myself were so moved by the breathless toil of our animals that we dismounted at a safe place, and walked. In five minutes we were in a worse condition than the horses; our knees tottered, our bodies were drenched with sweat, our eyes dim, heads giddy, and lungs utterly collapsed. At every tenth step we were obliged to pause in order to breathe, and after not more than three hundred steps I defied the Society for the Prevention of Cruelty to Animals, and mounted again. I am no light weight, and therefore it was Cruelty to Man (which is worse) to carry one's self up such a steep. I think we must have climbed in this style for a mile and a half; it seemed interminable. Then the angle of ascent fell off very greatly; the fir forest grew thick around us, shutting off the view of valley and mountains, and heaps of rotten snow began to appear in shady places. Where the trail had been shovelled out of drifts a month ago, we now rode over moist earth, between dripping, crumbling walls of snow. Another quarter of an hour, and the steeps fell back in front, leaving a lovely Alpine meadow, dotted with clumps of pine, the vivid green of its turf sprinkled with snowy star-flowers, and a brook of icy crystal winding through it.

I was delighted when Mr. Byers gave the word to un-saddle. It was barely three quarters of a mile, he said, to the summit of the Pass; whether we could cross was still a doubtful matter; and, before attempting it, both beasts and men must be fed. The former were turned loose to graze at will, with their long lariats dragging after them; the latter unhooked the cups from their button-holes, opened the coffee-bags, cut the ham with hunting-knives, and partook of the biscuits which were not sufficiently " sad." The water of the brook was so intensely cold that it almost made one scream. Yet immediately out of and through it grew clusters of a flower so purely beautiful that we all cried out with admiration on discovering it. Out of a ring of broadly ovate leaves (under the water) rose a straight stem twelve to fifteen inches in height, crowned at the top with a cluster of dark crimson-velvet flowers, about the size and with the rich mealy bloom of the polyanthus. It is called, here, the " Alpine primrose; " but I know of neither cowslip nor primrose that will com-pare with it. The odor is very peculiar, resembling that of Russia leather. Here is a treasure for our florists!

While we took our lunch and rested our bones Mr. Byers and White discussed the passage of the mountains. Di-rectly in front of us a depression in the fir-clad ridge indi-cated the summit of the Pass, on either side of which bald, snowy peaks rose considerably above the timber line. White had crossed the range last week, with a drove of twenty-two government horses; but he had gone consider-ably to the northward of the Pass, in order to avoid the snows. It was a question whether we should try to reopen the old trail, or follow his example and climb the frightful-looking steep on our right to a point beyond the timber. Being a green hand, I said nothing; but I felt relieved

when the Pass was selected, for the snows had been melting very rapidly, and I was convinced that we could falsify
the predictions of our friends.

The horses were saddled, the mules repacked, and we
set out upon the uncertain adventure. There was snow
all around us, — some drifts, even, lay on the meadow, —
and, even where it had melted, the soil was such an elastic,
treacherous bog, that we did not venture to ride. On all
sides rills came rushing down, uprooted trees barred the
way, or pools of black mud had collected. It was impossible to follow the trail, although we could trace it by the
marks of the shovels. Slowly, in single file, stopping every
two minutes to lean upon our horses' necks and gasp for
breath, spattered with mud and wet with snow-water, we
climbed through the forest, taking heart from the knowledge
that this was our last hard pull. The trees rapidly grew
thinner, the roaring rills became noiseless threads of water,
the snow-drifts overlapped each other and must be waded,
and then — the steep suddenly flattened, and a keen wind
blew over the summit of the Pass.

It is a sharp crest, with not ten yards between the opposite declivities. Here there was an open space, covered
with bunch-grass, among the fields of snow. We were
just at the limit of timber, a little more than eleven
thousand feet above the sea-level. No general panorama
of the range is visible, but there are inclosed views to the
east and west. Behind us, a sweep of bleak, frosty summits, too near (apparently), too hard and sharp, to be beautiful. Before us, far away over the deeps of endless dark-
green forest, a grand Alpine range,

> " lifting there
> A thousand shadow-pencilled valleys
> And snowy dells in a golden air."

Still further, thirty or forty miles behind it, arose two great
snowy pyramids, evidently beyond the North Park, and not
inferior in height to Mont Blanc. This view was superior,

in all the elements of sublimity, to anything I had seen since entering the mountains. In the centre of the bare spot where we gathered grew a ranunculus, a blossom of which I transferred to my note-book.

Beyond us, on the Pacific slope, we could see nothing but a waste of snow. Our two mountaineers, therefore, determined to make a preliminary exploration. Plunging into the drifts, wherein they sank to their thighs at nearly every step, they disappeared from sight, while we discussed the chances of reaching the Park before night. It was now two o'clock in the afternoon, the distance somewhere between twelve and fifteen miles, and unknown hardships and perils on the way — by no means an encouraging prospect! In half an hour Mr. Byers and White made their appearance, very much fagged and not particularly cheerful. The former simply said, — " We 'll try it ! " and took his horse's bridle. We followed, keeping the pack-mules near the centre of the line, and commenced the descent.

The snow, we soon found, was of very irregular texture. After walking three or four steps on the surface, we would suddenly plunge into a loose, melting mass, men and horses floundering together. It was necessary to lead by a long rein, to avoid the leaps and struggles of the latter. Where the descent was steep, I frequently found myself buried nearly to the hips and thrown upon my face, with the horse's head resting on my back. Now and then a rock, a log, or the top of a sharp knoll offered us a resting-place, and the chance of shaking off the snow, the penetrative cold of which pierced to one's very marrow. In one place there was a gulf of snow overhanging an arrowy torrent. I cleared it with a leap, and then, as my mare prepared to follow, took a second leap, to give her room to land. For a moment she hung by her forefeet, but a strong pull on the bridle brought her out of the danger. The dry, horny branches of the firs were also to be avoided; they both stabbed and tore, and in our headlong plunges it was not easy to keep out of their way. After nearly a mile of this travel, when strength, hope, and courage were on the point of giving out, the drifts diminished, and we could now and then walk in a bog of black mud, which was a pleasant relief. A little further, and Mr. Byers announced that the trail was found, although not yet practicable — we must still break our own way.

Our faces were smarting and our throats were parched, yet the snow-water, which set our teeth on edge with its coldness, did not seem to quench thirst in the least. We were soon enabled, however, to mount, and throw the burden of fatigue on the horses. After a short but very steep descent, the path was barred by an impetuous torrent, which was crossed at one point by a frail arch of snow left from a drift. White boldly walked over, leading his horse after him; but no one else dared to follow. After a little search we found a fordable place, and crossed, with the water foaming up to our saddles. There was yet another branch of the same river before us, and this proved to be both deeper and swifter. Mr. Beard's mule tottered and gave way, but regained his footing just on the brink of a rapid, and with a little care we all got safely over.

We were now able to follow the trail, except where it led into boggy holes, where the horses frequently sank to their bellies. On account of the fallen timber, it was a work of considerable difficulty to get around these holes. An interminable forest surrounded us. During the first four or five miles, we had an occasional glimpse of open green meadows on our right, and spurs of the snowy range towering beyond; afterwards, nothing but a dark wilderness of pines, firs, and aspens. The descent was very gradual — so much so, that after travelling for three hours, we were still in the midst of snow-drifts. My boots were completely sodden, and my feet and legs soon became so icy cold that I was forced to walk a good part of the way, although the exercise seemed to rack every joint in the body.   Mile after mile and hour after hour passed by, and still the same gloomy, dreary forest ; still snow, mud-holes, and fallen logs.   We had forced the Berthoud Pass, and expected to camp in the Park, which was cause for congratulation ; but how devoutly we longed for the valley to open !

A break in the wood showed us the evening shadows high on the opposite mountain.   The air was already damp and chill, and the open, level portion of the Park was yet two miles distant.   All at once the trail entered a meadow of deep grass, two acres in extent, and our leader dismounted under a clump of trees.   Mr. Beard and myself rolled out of our saddles, ungirthed, turned the animals loose, and then threw ourselves down before the fire (which had been immediately kindled), too fatigued to be very conscious of rest.   It was very fortunate that Mr. Sumner has a talent for cooking ; had the meal depended on either of us, I fear it would have been of the " square " order.   A pot of coffee — hot, black, and strong — soon circulated among us, a veritable lubricating oil to stiff joints, and an anodyne to bruised muscles.

There were no songs and stories around the camp-fire. Each one made haste to find a portion of the earth's surface as little lumpy as possible, and dispose his blankets with a view to warmth and comfort.   The artist and I united our stock of bedding, and I added a mattress of fir boughs, but we had little comfort during the night.   The mosquitoes were plentiful, the noises of the animals disturbed us, and toward morning it became wretchedly cold. The meadow was flooded with splendid moonlight, and whenever I opened my eyes on the mysterious mazes of light and gloom in the depth of the forest, I became excited and restless.   It seemed a long while until the chilly dawn arrived ; but then, the last nap I took, while somebody else was kindling the fire, refreshed me more than all the broken sleep of the night.

XII.

CAMP NEAR BLUE RIVER, MIDDLE PARK, *July* 1, 1866.

OUR first morning in camp found us sore, stiff, and but half refreshed after the hardships of crossing the Pass. Nevertheless, we breakfasted, saddled, packed, and got under way with alacrity, encouraged by the prospect of a restorative bath at the Hot Springs, which are said to heal all sorts of ailments, bring the hair to bald heads, and put new blood into old veins.

The trail bore away to the left of Frazer River, over gently undulating ground, still wooded; but the trees were smaller, the soil dry, and the increasing gleams of sky through the topmost boughs indicated that we were getting out of the mountains. On the way we found a geranium — pink, veined with purple; a beautiful orchid, almost identical with the cyclamen of Italy and Greece; violets; rose-colored *pogonias*, with a delicate, peach-blossom odor; and huge beds of a snow-white, golden-hearted star-flower. The occasional openings among the pines were natural gardens, which I regretted to see trampled upon by the hoofs of our beasts.

After riding thus for half an hour, there was an exclamation from the foremost of the party. The long, long forest was at an end; we found ourselves at the head of a superb meadow stretching westward for five or six miles; bounded on the north, first by low gray hills of fantastic shape, then by great green ascending slopes of forest, and above all, jagged ranges of rock and snow. On the south were low

swells of pine and aspen, near at hand; twenty miles behind them detached spurs of mountains, conspicuous among
which rose a lofty wedge-like peak.   Although on the Pacific slope of the Rocky Mountains, the dividing ridge, or
water-shed between the two oceans, embraced us on three
sides.   The main chain meanders through Colorado in a
curiously tortuous course.   It comes down the west side of
the North Park (which is drained by the head-waters of
the North Platte) ; then turns directly eastward, separating
the North from the Middle Park; then southward, bound-
ing the Middle Park (the waters of which flow to the Colorado and the Californian Gulf) on the east; then due westward, dividing the Middle from the South Park (which
collects and unites the waters of the *South* Platte) ; and
finally, after making an abrupt curve around the head-waters of the Arkansas, strikes southward toward New Mexico.
The Parks form a very remarkable feature of the mountain
region.   They resemble, on a smaller scale, the lofty, moun-
tain-bounded table-lands of Cashmere and Thibet.   They
are still but imperfectly explored, and still more imperfectly
represented on the maps.   I have not been able to find any
minute description of their scenery, soil, and climate ;
hence, every step of the present journey has been full of
interest.   In fact, none of the accounts of travel among
the Rocky Mountains seem to me to present their *individuality*, as mountains, very distinctly — to discriminate between what is original, and peculiar to them, and those
general features which all mountain regions possess in
common.   Each day, thus far, has brought me its new
surprises ; but I shall content myself, at present, with giving the details of the journey.

The change from the forest to this meadow was that from
confinement to liberty.   Our animals seemed to feel it also,
and trotted forward briskly through the thick green grass.
Near the head of the meadow we passed a large hay-stack
and squatter's shanty, where the horses pastured in the

Park are fed during the winter. Only one man — Jones, who discovered the new pass — has attempted to establish a ranche. He has sowed sixty acres of grain on the lower part of Grand River, but White informs me that the attempt does not promise much. The average level of the Park above the sea cannot be less than eight thousand feet. Although the extreme of cold is not so great as in Denver, the winter is so long, and the summer nights so cool, that it is doubtful whether grain (except barley and oats) can be raised.

My lean mare was evidently not adequate to the task ; so White, catching sight of a herd of horses and mules, near the further end of the meadow, promised me an Indian pony in exchange, and rode off in advance to drive in the herd. The animals, like those we had taken from Empire, belong to Charley Utter, whom we had hoped to have as a companion for the journey ; but he had joined the rush of gold-hunters for Bear River (a hundred miles west of the Middle Park), and had not yet returned. Mr. Beard, also, groaned over his McClellan saddle, and the gait of his mule. We both, therefore, looked forward with some impatience to the noonday halt.

After crossing a number of swift, swollen streams which came down from the left, we reached a higher and dryer part of the meadow, and the strong, juicy grass gave place to sage-bush and flowers — a plain of silver-gray, sprinkled with a myriad minute dots of color. The odor which filled the air was so exquisite as slightly to intoxicate the senses. For miles I seemed to be riding through a Turkish bazaar, and inhaling the mingled scent of cloves, sandal-wood, and attar of roses. My aches and cramps were forgotten : I swam in an atmosphere of balm, half narcotized with the rich, voluptuous delight of breathing it.

White started up a very large fox, which was cunning enough to keep out of rifle-range. We skirted the wood on the left, and left the meadow for a low, dry plateau, which was one mile-long bed of blue larkspurs and scarlet star-wort. The grazing animals had been added to our *caballada*, and we sped merrily along the trail, increasing the breadth and sweep of our panoramic landscapes, as we penetrated deeper into the hilly region. I exchanged my mare for a tough little yellow Indian pony, barefooted, but nimble and intelligent: after inspecting me with his nose, and apparently finding no objection, he established confidential relations at once, and has served me, thus far, with unswerving fidelity.

It was a singular country through which we rode, and I regret that I am not able to describe its geological character. Hills wooded with aspen, and narrow, grassy dells, alternated with wide sweeps of irregular table-land, treeless and bare, except for a growth of sage and larkspur. The valleys of the larger streams which thread the Middle Park were shut out from view, but the distant cincture of Alpine summits met the eye, in every direction. We rode twenty miles, — two thirds of the distance to the Hot Springs, — made a brief noon-camp beside a brook, and then pushed forward again toward a lofty range of hills which arose before us.

Gradually, all the eastern portion of the Park came into view. I readily distinguished the Berthoud Pass, as well as that at the head of Clear Creek, and could roughly measure by the eye both their elevation above the Park and the character of the approaches which they offer for a railroad. On this side of the mountains there seems to be no difficulty, except such as might arise from heavy snows during the winter. To the northeast Mr. Byers pointed out the Bowlder Pass, which rises above the timber line, but is almost bare of snow. It is practicable for wagons, but is very little travelled. An isolated chimney rock, two or three hundred feet in height, stands like a beacon on the very summit of this pass.

I can add to my own Mr. Beard's testimony as to the

originality of the Park scenery, in an artistic point of view.
The features are large and broad, with outlines to some
extent fantastic, yet not inharmonious. In color, gray pre-
dominates, but a gray most rare in landscape, — silvery over
the sage-plains, greenish and pearly along the slopes of
bunch-grass, and occasionally running into red where the
soil shows through the thin vegetation. In the grand views
— fifty miles in extent — from the ridge we were climbing,
there were no positive tints, but the most delicate and surprising succession of broad half-tints, to which sunshine
and cloud-shadows lent the loveliest effect. The brush
only can describe landscapes so new in character. I found
myself thinking of Central Asia, — of the regions of Ko-
kand and Kashgar, as I imagine them to be. From this
point, there were no forests, except aspen groves, on the
crests of the hills ; the gray undulations swept into the
distance, dipping here and there into hollows of singular
form, and leaning, far away, against the feet of mountain-
ranges, where there was the faint green glimmer of a meadow at the foot of every snowy ravine. The flushed snows
of the farther summits did not seem lofty and inaccessible,
— our own elevation reduced the highest of them to less
than seven thousand feet,— but their irregular character and
great variety of outline gave the true background for such
landscapes.

The animals occasioned us much trouble during this
day's journey. Our little black pack-mule, Peter, has a
diabolical knack of shifting his load, so that the proper
balance is lost, and the pack-saddle turns. On one of
these occasions, while White and I were engaged in re-
packing, Mr. Beard rode up and offered his services. It was
fortunate that we did not need them, for he afterward confessed that he had tried to dismount, and (in consequence
of the previous day's hardships) was unable to do so. I
was in scarcely better plight, but had no reason to complain ; I had been wishing for severe physical fatigue, and

now I have it in abundance. We were obliged to drive with us an Arapahoe mare, belonging to the new herd, and a more outrageous creature never grazed. By some sort of animal magnetism, she immediately took command of all our horses and mules, and yet never lost an opportunity of biting, kicking, and driving them from the trail. The more violent her behavior toward them, the more they were fascinated with her. Her vicious eyes were always on the lookout; while we watched her all was quiet, but the moment we became absorbed in scenery or some topic of conversation, she would dash at one of the animals and break up the line of march. White confessed that she had exasperated him to such a pitch that he shot at her, and was now sorry that he missed.

Gradually climbing the hills, among beds of crimson and violet lupins, scarlet star-flowers, and many showy unknown plants, we came at last to a divide, whence the trail sloped down to the valley of Grand River at the Hot Springs, now four miles distant. Mr. Byers pointed out a bluff, covered with scattering clumps of red cedar, as the objective point of our day's journey. On our right towered a lofty ridge, thrusting out buttresses of perpendicular rock, crowned with pines; and beyond the Grand River arose a similar, but much grander and more abrupt formation. Between the two the river issued, winding away westward among green, interlocking hills, until we could only guess its gate-way out of the Park among some snow-peaks, thirty or forty miles away.

The prospect of a sulphur-bath helped us over the re-mainder of the way, and in another hour we dismounted in a meadow on the banks of the Grand River, directly opposite to the Hot Springs. Mr. Byers looked at the stream, and meditated; White did the same thing. It was fluid ice (for coldness), forty or fifty yards wide, swift as an arrow, and evidently too deep to ford. On the opposite bank we saw a rough log-cabin, on a little knoll, and a stream of white, smoking water tumbling down a rock, ten feet high, in a smoking pool below. Forms were moving among some cotton-woods on the river bottom; their red blankets announced that they were Indians. While we were hesitating, some rheumatic eremite whom White knew, came down to the bank, and with much difficulty shouted across above the roar of the water, that it was impossible to cross; we must go eight miles higher up the river. (But eight miles on the opposite side meant fifteen on ours.) Two of us, at least, were in no mood to remount that day, and the rest of the party did not seem very enthusiastic.

It was finally decided that we should camp where we were, and those who wished to visit the Hot Springs should swim the river. White and I stripped to our shirts and drawers, mounted our animals bare-backed, and rode down to the water. While we were trying to force them in, they refusing with all their might, we were again hailed from the other side, and warned against making the attempt. A short distance below us the river entered a cañon, and became a cataract. This fact, combined with the fearful coldness and swiftness of the current, made us pause. It was no doubt well that we did so, — well that we silently turned and rode back to the camp. All I can say of the Hot Springs, therefore, is, that they gush from the earth in a stream almost large enough to turn a mill; that they make a smoking cascade, with a hot pool below; that they are said to work wonderful cures; and that two gentlemen dispute the priority of preëmpting them.

There we were, on the bare plain, without a tree for shelter, our only fuel the rubbish left from former camp-fires, and a black thunder-storm coming up. Turning the horses loose to drag their lariats and graze, we first kindled a fire, and then set about securing our baggage from the rain. Forming a sort of platform with fragments of wood, we placed our blankets and sacks thereon, and covered them with india-rubber cloth.   Mr. Beard was at great pains to find a place for his umbrella under the water-proof; and not until the storm was over, leaving us half-soaked, did it occur to him that he might have used it!   Fortunately, there was more wind and thunder than rain, and the superb indigo-gray of the mountains in shadow repaid us for the drenching.   Toward evening, it became very evident that the Arapahoe mare was slyly leading our animals out of our view, in order to make off with them.   White trudged away through the wet grass and brought them back; but it was necessary, moreover, to catch and picket the mare.

It was easier to decide that this should be done, than to do it.   The mare was separated from the other animals, and driven into a corner of the meadow between the river and the bluffs at the entrance of the cañon.   One of the gentlemen then took his stand above, while White cautiously approached with a lariat.   Skill and strategy were alike in vain; with a whirl and a dash she avoided the flying noose, and shot off between her pursuers.   Others went to the rescue, and the scene soon became very exciting. All the other horses and mules left off grazing, drew near, and watched the contest with the most absorbed interest. It was perfectly evident that they understood this was to be a test of power, settling the question whether they were to be ruled by us or the mare.   They were politicians on the fence, and reminded us of newspapers and individuals, who and which shall be nameless.   To watch them was to me the most interesting part of the spectacle; they followed every movement of men and mare, standing knee-deep in rich grass which they never thought of cropping. It was nearly an hour before the provoking beast was finally cornered, noosed, and tied to a tree.   The other animals then turned away and went to their grazing, paying not the slightest heed to her.   She was nobody, now that she could no longer kick nor patronize.   Then I thought of certain political leaders.

White's rage was not yet allayed. He took a piece of sapling, and laid it heavily on the mare's hide. Then he came back and sat down by the fire, declaring that she should have no pasture that night. Half an hour passed; the rest of the herd were luxuriating on the meadow, while the culprit, sore and hungry, hung her head dejectedly beside the tree. White arose, stole quietly away, made a picket, brought the mare down to the meadow, and fastened her in good pasture. "She looked kind o' pitiful," he said.

We made our bed on the wet earth, expecting to be rained upon during the night; but the heavens were merciful, and we enjoyed sound and tolerably dry sleep. I experienced three distinct electric shocks, probably from the fact that I was insulated by the india-rubber cloth upon which I lay, and then touched the earth with my hand. On the snowy ranges persons are sometimes so charged, that there are sparks and crackling sounds at every movement of their bodies. Men unacquainted with the phenomenon imagine that bees have gotten into their hair and that rattlesnakes are at their heels. Many strange stories are told of the effect of the fluid, which seems to manifest itself in an eccentric but not a dangerous form.

XIII.

BRECKENRIDGE, BLUE RIVER, *July* 2, 1866.

WE arose from our moist couch on the banks of Grand
River, to find the stream still rising, and a thick mist, fore-
boding rain, spread over the face of the earth. Mr. Byers's
friend, Dr. Wharton, who was encamped at the Springs,
came down to the opposite bank, and some notes, tied to
stones, were exchanged. I received in this way a pink
malva, which made the airy journey without damage. Our
further route gave rise to a serious consultation. In three
days more I had appointed to be in Breckenridge, at the
head of Blue River, about seventy-five miles from the
Springs. There was no probability that we could ford the
Blue, in the present swollen condition of all the mountain
streams, and the regular trail lay beyond that river. We
were aware, indeed, that the Ute Indians made use of
another trail on this side, striking directly across the Middle Park (the diameter of which is nearly a hundred
miles), but none of our party had ever traversed it, or
knew anything about it beyond the rumor that it was exceedingly difficult and dangerous.

Yet there was no alternative — we were limited to the
choice of this unknown route. It was a matter of great
regret that we had failed in reaching the Hot Springs, and
I proposed to start for Breckenridge in company with
White, leaving the rest of the party to cross the Grand at
the upper ford if they preferred. They decided, however,
that we should keep together, and we made immediate
preparations for departure.

7

We first retraced our trail for two miles or more, then, turning westward, crossed a high ridge wooded with aspen, and descended toward the Grand over aromatic slopes of sage-bush.   The mist rolled into clouds and hid all the higher mountains from view, — which I greatly regretted, as from this point we might have seen the Rabbit-Ears — two remarkable Alpine horns on the western border of the North Park.   We struck the Grand in the cañon below the Springs, and for some distance the path was notched along the side of a fir-wooded steep, over the roaring flood. Small brooks, invisible under dense willow thickets, came down on our left, making deep side-dells in the bluff.   It was not very far, however, before the cañon opened, revealing a broad gray landscape, through which the Grand could be traced into the distance by its belt of cotton-woods.

We rode forward over what is called the "second bottom" — a low table-land, rising into hills a mile from the river, covered with a uniform growth of silvery sage, and dotted with grazing antelope.   The sun came out, the mist arose from the snowy ranges, and all aspects were cheerful except the company of the Arapahoe mare, which, thank Heaven! was not to last long.   We heard the cry of an eagle circling in the air over our heads, and had not proceeded half a mile further before we discovered an eagle's. nest in the top of a cotton-wood, just under the edge of the bluff.   We were able to ride within a hundred feet and look into it.   Three eaglets — awkward, owlish creatures, completely covered with thick gray down — sat on the edges of the nest, which was a huge structure of sticks, and yelped piteously.   It was a rare piece of good fortune for all of us, none of whom had ever seen (and probably will never see again) an eagle's nest with the brood in it. Mr. Beard, with the aid of a good glass, made a permanent acquisition ; and when his picture is exhibited, I can testify that he paints what he has seen.

Williams Fork,—or, as it is better called, Roaring Fork,

— a large affluent of the Grand, now announced itself in front, by the tops of its timber rising above the bluff. It was also much swollen, and the fording was a matter of some difficulty. Mr. Byers, as usual, led the way, breasting the icy water, which, striking his horse's side, almost swept over its back. We all took an extremely cold leg-bath, and my pony came within an ace of being carried down the stream. On the opposite bank we divided our party, White taking the spare animals (including the Arapahoe mare) to Charley Utter's cabin, five miles further down the Grand, while the rest of us determined to try the Ute trail, up the west bank of Roaring Fork. This arrangement would save us several miles of the journey, as White, on his strong mule, could easily rejoin us during the afternoon. Somewhere ahead of us lay the famous moss-agate region, which we were especially desirous of visiting, each one having his private hopes of jewelry for wife or sweetheart.

The soil on the narrow bottoms of Roaring Fork is the purest *humus*, producing grass of astonishing rankness and richness, which our animals snapped at with crazy eagerness. We had not proceeded a mile, however, before our way was barred by an abrupt mountain, through the centre of which the stream forced its way, in a narrow, rock-walled slit — a *cañon* (funnel) in the strictest sense of the word. The trail led us into this cleft, taking the very edge of a precipice two hundred feet in perpendicular depth, where there was barely room for our horses to set their hoofs. Under us the river was a mass of foam: opposite — not a stone's throw across — rose the jagged walls of dark-red rock, terminating in fantastic pinnacles. It was an exciting passage, not unmixed with fear, especially when the disarrangement of a saddle in advance forced Mr. Beard and myself to halt for five minutes in the narrowest part of the pass, where portions of the rock under us had crumbled away.

A valley succeeded; then a second and loftier range, where the dividing cañon disclosed the most singular formations of rock — natural fortresses and towers. One trail wound away to the right; another (possibly an old elk-path) seemed to lead directly into the gorge. The former was preferable, on account of the pack-mules; but Mr. McCandless and myself determined to try the latter, believing that we might gain in time what we lost in laborious travel. The ascent was so steep, that we could with difficulty keep our foothold in climbing; and it was wonderful to see the confidence which the horses had in our leadership and the dexterity with which they followed us. My pony used his hoofs as I did my hands, taking hold of grass-tufts and projections of rock, and resting with his nose on my shoulder when I stopped to take breath. Huge, detached masses of rock and bushes prevented our having a good view of the chasm, but the general wildness and picturesqueness of the scenery was an ample repayment for our toil. From the highest part of the Pass another grand gray landscape opened to the southward, magnificently bounded by a dark-green mountain chain, every summit of which was a jagged pyramid of snow.

After half an hour of rather laborious scrambling, I reached the grassy meadow beyond the cañon. Looking back, I saw the others of the party slowly creeping over a mountain ridge a mile or more to the west. I thereupon struck a diagonal course, and presently came upon the Indian trail, on the "second bottom." Here the ground was strewn with rough agates, but with all my search I could find no mossy specimens. When the others arrived, in the course of half an hour, I found that their experience had been precisely similar. Our dreams of complete sets of jewelry diminished to a single brooch or ring, and then faded into the thin atmosphere of disappointed hopes. None of us found a single moss-agate.

Here and there on the trail we could detect the marks

of lodge-poles, which, we supposed, were made by the Utes in passing from Blue to Grand River. As this was our only guidance through the unknown portion of the Park, we followed it, although its general direction seemed too much east of south. The mountain range in front was apparently a spur thrust out from the south into the very heart of the Park, and we must cross it in order to reach the Valley of Blue River. The government maps were of no assistance, — they omitted the mountains, and inserted streams which have no existence. Directly in front of us towered a splendid peak, not less than fourteen thousand feet in height; and there seemed to be no practicable pass across the range except immediately on either side of it : so long, therefore, as our trail tended toward it, we could not go very far astray. It was about twenty miles to the base of the range, the intermediate country being a mixture of rich, grassy valleys, sage-clad table-land, and picturesque, broken hills, flecked with groves of aspen and fir.

We started up several sage-hens, with their broods of young. They are a kind of grouse, about the size of the prairie-chicken, and of gray, mottled plumage. Their color seems to be their chief protection, as was shown by their reliance upon it. The young birds scarcely took the trouble to get out of our way, and one of them was caught sitting under a sage-bush, and looking with bright, un-shrinking eyes directly in the face of its captor. Of course we did not shoot the hens, — an act of self-denial (our salt fare being considered) which ought to be set down to our credit. Ere long we reached meadows again, threaded by swift tributary brooks of the Roaring Fork. The passage of these streams, small as they were, gave us some trouble, owing to the treacherous character of the soil. Mr. Beard's mule went down and rolled over upon him, pinning him fast in the mud, and my pony only avoided a like disaster by his great shrewdness and agility.

At one o'clock we camped on the banks of a brook, and

our fishers immediately got their gear in readiness for trout. Two of us determined on a bath in spite of mosquitoes and ice-water; and while a portion of the party were playing leap-frog *solitaire*, in the search for grasshopper bait, another portion landing an occasional diminutive fish, and the remainder attempting to dry their tingling skins, there was a sudden cry of "How, how!" across the low willow thickets. Indians, with vermilion faces and streaming black hair! There were two braves and squaws, mounted, and two pappooses. They crossed to us without ceremony, shook hands, and attempted conversation, which was not very edifying until we discovered that one of them understood a little Spanish. We then learned that they were on their way from the Blue to join the remainder of their tribe on the head-waters of the Grand; their chief, Colorado, was at Breckenridge, and they thought the rivers could be forded. One of the men — who wore, singularly enough, an *Austrian* military coat (from Maximilian's army?) — possessed some tact and discretion. He prevented the other from going too near our luggage, and withdrew with him to a little distance when we sat down to our meal. He showed a little curiosity about a satchel of mine; but when I told him it was "medicine," and made certain mysterious signs, he seemed satisfied. The squaws brought their shy pappooses to look at us — beautiful beings, all of them, with paint-smeared faces, and hideously suggestive hair and blankets. Uncas and Cora, — heroes and heroines of romance!

Presently another horseman appeared, galloping toward us over the hills, from the opposite direction. It was White, who, to our great joy, had a sage-hen at his saddle-bow, and a supply of antelope-venison for our supper. He, too, had crossed a corner of the moss-agate patch, without finding any of the jewels. Considerably refreshed by the bath and by *one* delicious trout apiece, (would it had been a dozen!) we pushed forward, entering a hilly region, where dense tracts of woodland alternated with fields of flowers. The tracks of elk, deer, and even bear, were frequent, but much as our hunters dashed away from the trail, they brought us nothing.   After some miles, we found ourselves suddenly on a bluff, overlooking Roaring Fork, which issued, with many a snaky twist, from a stretch of pine forest.   Into this forest went the trail, so obstructed with fallen timber that our progress was an unintermitted series of leaps.   We outdid all the performances that were ever made with bars in the circus-ring.

On emerging from this wood we found ourselves in the loveliest meadow-park, several miles long, opening before us directly to the foot of the great snowy peak.   A swift brook sped down it, under bowery thickets and past clumps of trees; the turf was brilliantly green and spangled with flowers; low hills bounded it on either side, the forests with which they were covered sending out irregular capes, and arms embracing bays of grass; and over the sweet pastoral seclusion towered the Alpine chain, here smitten with gold by the sinking sun, there glooming broad and blue under the shadows of thunder-clouds.   Nothing could have been more unexpected than the change from aspen woods and silvery hills of sage to this green, pine-enframed, Arcadian landscape.   We made our camp for the night in a grove of trees, which our huge fire of pine-logs illuminated with magical effect.   Moreover, we had fresh meat for the first time, couches on a matting of pine needles, the best of pasturage for our beasts, and for the first time since leaving Empire, enjoyed a feeling of comfort.   It rained during the night, but the trees made a partial shelter.   Our day's travel could not have been less than thirty miles.

It was now very evident that the pass we sought lay to the right of the high peak, and that the Valley of the Blue was beyond the range.   The majestic mountain has no name.   It is very near the centre of the Middle Park, and its summit must command a view of this whole inclosed region. I therefore suggest that it be called Park Peak (rather than such a name as Cummings or Doolittle), and — if no one has any objection — will so designate it.

We soon reached the head of the meadow, where a jungle of willow-bushes, threaded by a net-work of streams, lay between us and the mountain. The trail was wet and boggy, and the dripping boughs through which we forced our way, wet us to the skin. Then ensued a horrible scramble, which lasted for nearly two miles. We either floundered in mud in the bottom of a glen, climbed over piles of fallen timber, or crept up and down slippery, crumbling staircases, of loose soil. In such places our pack-mules showed a wonderful talent. The skill with which they passed between trees, leaped logs, and steadied themselves along the edge of ticklish declivities, without disarranging their packs, could never be imagined by one who had not seen it. We considered these two miles equal to ten of good road. The trail gradually improved, and we entered a region, which was a perfect reproduction of the mountain-dells of Saxony. Meadows of velvet turf lay embedded in tall, dark forests of fir, which stretched up the slopes above us until they formed a fringe against the sky. At every winding of the valley, I looked, involuntarily, for the old, mossy mill, and the squares of bleaching linen on the grass. Snow-drifts made their appearance where the shade was deepest, and the few aspens and alders were just putting forth their leaves.

This part of the Pass was so beautiful, that we reached the summit — much sooner than we expected — almost with regret. We had not risen more than a thousand feet above the general level of the Park. From the top we looked down a narrow, winding glen, between lofty parapets of rock, and beheld mountains in the distance, dark with shadow, and vanishing in clouds. The descent was steep, but not very toilsome. After reaching the bed of the glen, we followed it downward through beds of grass and flowers,

under the shade of castellated rocks, and round the feet
of natural ramparts, until it opened upon wide plains of
sage-bush, which formed the shelving side of an immense
valley. The usual line of cotton-wood betrayed a stream,
and when we caught a glimpse of the water, its muddy tint
— the sure sign of gold-washing — showed that we had
found the Blue River. We had crossed the Ute Pass, as
it is called by the trappers, and are among the first white
men who have ever traversed it. We now looked on Park
Peak from the west side.

Instead of descending to the river, our trail turned southward, running nearly parallel with its course, near the top
of the sloping plane which connects the mountains with the
valley. The sun came out, the clouds lifted and rolled
away, and one of the most remarkable mountain landscapes
of the earth was revealed to our view. The Valley of the
Blue, which, for a length of thirty miles, with a breadth
varying from five to ten, lay under our eyes, wore a tint of
pearly silver-gray, upon which the ripe green of the timber
along the river, and the scattered gleams of water seemed
to be enamelled. Opposite to us, above this sage-color, rose
huge mountain-foundations, where the grassy openings were
pale, the forests dark, the glens and gorges filled with
shadow, the rocks touched with lines of light — making a
chequered effect that suggested cultivation and old settlement. Beyond these were wilder ridges, all forest; then
bare masses of rock, streaked with snow, and, highest of
all, bleak snow-pyramids, piercing the sky. From south to
north stretched the sublime wall — the western boundary
of the Middle Park; and where it fell away toward the
cañon by which Grand River goes forth to seek the Colorado, there was a vision of dim, rosy peaks, a hundred
miles distant. In breadth of effect — in airy depth and
expansion — in simple yet most majestic outline, and in
originality yet exquisite harmony of color, this landscape is
unlike anything I have ever seen. I feel how inadequate

are my words to suggest such new combinations of tints and forms. There is greater *vertical* grandeur among the Alps : here it is the vast *lateral* extent which impresses you, together with the atmospheric effect occasioned by great elevation above the sea. You stand on the plane of the Alpine glaciers ; a new vegetation surrounds you ; a darker sky is over your head ; yet the grand picture upon which you look is complete in all its parts, or, if any element is wanting, its absence is swallowed up in the majesty that is present.

"If Gifford were only here!" said Beard; and did not take out his own sketch-book.

We enjoyed this landscape for several miles, until the hills, reaching across the valley, formed a cañon, to avoid which we crossed spurs which shut everything but the snowy range. The base of Park Peak, on our right, offered many picturesque features ; but I will not attempt to describe them. Other snowy summits appeared before us, overlooking the head of Blue River Valley ; charming valleys opened among the nearer mountains ; yet the remembrance of what we had seen made us indifferent to them. In the afternoon we came upon several lodges of Utes, one of which I entered, not without misgivings. The occupant was a sharp, shrewd Indian, who wanted to trade a buckskin for much more powder than it was worth. There were but two men at home, but a number of squaws and children. A herd of rough ponies was grazing near. We found little to interest us, and presently left Mr. Low (Low, the poor Indian, as the people here say) to his own devices.

A mile or two further we came to a swift stream, which we supposed to be Snake River, and the prospect of trout was so promising that, after effecting a crossing, we encamped for the night, calculating that we were within fifteen miles of this place. Hunters and fishers went forth, while the artist and myself tried both pencil and pen with little effect. We agreed that we were demoralized by fatigue, and that lying on our blankets before the fire was better than either Art or Literature.

Though so near Breckenridge, we were not yet out of the woods, as my next will show.

XIV.

BUCKSKIN JOE, SOUTH PARK, *July* 3, 1866.

WHEN we awoke in our camp, on the banks of the river which we supposed to be Snake, yesterday morning, the ground was covered with a white frost, and the water remaining in our tin cups was turned to ice. To bathe a sun-blistered face on such a morning, is a torture rather than a luxury; yet the air was at once a tonic, a stimulant, and a flavor. The peaks across the valley — not much less than fifteen thousand feet in height — flashed in rosy splendor; the dew sprinkled with diamonds the silver of the sage-fields; the meadow-larks sang joyously, and our spirits rose with the belief that the uncertain portion of our journey was nearly over.

A ride of three miles up the valley brought us to another river — a fuller stream than the last, foaming down through a wild gap in the mountains on our left. At this place the Blue receives a considerable affluent on the opposite side — a circumstance which told us precisely where we were. The stream where we had encamped is still nameless; it was the Snake which we had now reached. We forded it with some difficulty, the water rushing over our saddles, and followed a barely discernible trail along the foot of the mountains. The Valley of the Blue became narrow, hemmed in by the feet of spurs from the main chain. The bottom-land was marshy and full of pools, and we were sometimes forced to climb around quagmires and fallen timber, at points of threatening steepness. Sometimes, also, a slide of rocks had come down from above, leaving piles over which the animals must slowly and cautiously be led. The little gray coneys sat on the stones above, and barked at us as we passed.

It is rather difficult to measure distance during travel of this kind; but I suppose we had made about three miles after fording Snake River, when the trail — or, rather, what was left of it — terminated at the Blue. There were signs that the stream had been crossed here, and as we had been looking with longing eyes at the pleasant open bottoms on the other side, we imagined our troubles at an end. Mr. McCandless plunged in, his mule breasting the impetuous current, and, after being carried down some yards, succeeded in getting out on the other bank. Mr. Byers followed, and then the pack-mule, Peter; but, on reaching the centre of the stream both were carried away. I was watching the horse, madly endeavoring to swim against the current, when there was a sudden call for help. The drift-timber had made a raft just below, the force of the stream set directly toward it, and horse and rider were being drawn, as it appeared, to inevitable destruction. Mr. Sumner sprang into the water and caught Mr. Byers's hand; but the next moment he was out of his depth, and barely succeeded in swimming ashore.

All this seemed to take place in a second. The river made a short curve around a little tongue of land, across which we sprang, in time to see Mr. Byers catch at and hold the branch of a drifted tree, in passing. In another moment he had extricated himself from the saddle. White rushed into the water with a lariat, and the danger was over. Horse and rider got out separately, without much trouble, although the latter was already chilled to the bones and nearly benumbed. The pack-mule, with all our luggage, was completely submerged, and we should probably have lost everything, had not White grasped the mule's ear at the turn of the river, and thus assisted the beast to recover his footing. It was all over before we were clearly aware of the full extent of the danger and of our own fears.

When the wet clothes had been wrung out, and the wet pistols fired, we set forward, compelled to follow the east bank of the Blue, with *no* trail. We had the choice between mud-holes and fallen timber, or a steep of loose gravel and sliding stones, which defied us to get a firm foothold. Thus we worked our way along, with almost incredible labor, for an hour or more, when we reached an overhanging rocky wall, at the foot of which the river foamed and roared in a narrow channel. When we had climbed around the rocks and reached the mountain side above, a fearful-looking slant of disintegrated shale, through which a few stunted aspen bushes grew, lay before us. One more degree of steepness would have made the pass impossible. The crumbled rock slid from under our feet, and rattled in showers from the brink of the precipice into the water below ; and but for the help which the bushes gave us in the worst places, we should probably have followed. Messrs. Byers and Davis, who were in advance, seemed at times to be hanging in the air. In the midst of this pass, a badger whisked around the corner of a rock, tempting one of the party to let himself down to the edge of the bluff in the hope of getting a shot ; but the animal was safe in some hole or crevice.

While resting among the roots of a pine-tree, which enabled me also to support my pony, I descried Mr. McCandless riding up the meadows beyond the river, with a mounted Indian on each side of him. I noticed, moreover, that the latter kept pace with him, and took pains to keep him between them. As they were Utes, there was no trouble to be feared, and we supposed they were guiding him toward Breckenridge. Beyond this perilous corner of the mountain we found a faint trail, with a promise of better travel ahead. Mr. Beard and White were in the rear, and it was amusing to watch them follow us, clinging for life to the

bushes and roots, while their animals, with more than human cunning, picked their way step by step, through the
sliding fragments.

A mile or two more, and a broad valley opened on our
left. A very muddy stream — which could be none other
than Swan River — came down it to join the Blue. Mr.
McCandless and one of the Indians here rode down to the
opposite bank and hailed us. The latter was the famous
Ute chief, Colorado ; he said we could now either ford the
Blue, or take a good trail to Breckenridge on our side of
the river. We chose the latter, and presently came in sight
of Delaware Flats — a collection of log-cabins, across the
open valley. Leaving them to the left, we struck toward
another settlement called Buffalo Flats ; both places are
inhabited by miners engaged in gulch washing. The cattle
pasturing on the grassy bottoms were a welcome sight, after
five days of savage Nature. I greeted a young fellow,
herding mules on horseback, with a very superfluous feeling of friendship ; for he made a short, surly answer, and
rode away.

Being now but four miles from Breckenridge, we spurred
our weary animals forward, taking a trail which led for a
long distance through a burned forest. It was scenery of
the most hideous character. Tens of thousands of charred
black poles, striped with white where the bark had sprung
off, made a wilderness of desolation which was worse than
a desert. The boughs had been almost entirely consumed ;
the sunshine and the blue of the sky were split into a myriad of parallel slices, which fatigued and distracted the eye,
until one almost became giddy in riding through. I cannot
recall any phase of mundane scenery so disagreeable as
this.

Finally the wood came to an end, and green meadows
and snowy peaks refreshed our eyes. Over ditches, heaps
of stone and gravel, and all the usual débris of gulch-mining, we rode toward some cabins which beckoned to us

through scattered clumps of pine. A flag-staff, with something white at half-mast; canvas-covered wagons in the
shade ; a long street of log-houses; signs of " Boarding,"
" Miner's Home," and " Saloon," and a motley group of
rough individuals, among whom we detected the beard of
our parted comrade and the blanket of the chief— such
was Breckenridge !

The place dates from 1860 — yet, of the five thousand
miners who flocked to this part of the Middle Park in that
year, probably not more than five hundred remain.   At
present there is a slight increase of life.   Some new cabins
are going up, and for some distance beyond the limits of
building one sees lots staked out, and signs displayed, —
" Preëmpted by —— ——." At the first house we reached,
we found a long table set for dinner, and a barrel of beer
on tap, which had come over the snowy range from Montgomery the previous day.   The host, Mr. Sutherland, sus-
pected our impatient hunger, and only delayed the meal
long enough to add the unexpected delicacy of oyster soup.
Then, taking the bugle with which he blew the signal for
the immortal Light Brigade to charge at Balaklava, he
made the notes of " Peas upon a trencher" ring over the
shanties of Breckenridge.   Since that splendid Crimean
episode, Mr. Sutherland and his bugle have done loyal service in a Colorado regiment.   I was glad of the chance
which made us almost the first guests of his new establishment — especially as his bounty in providing equals his
gallantry in fighting.

In strolling up the street, after dinner, I discovered that
the apparent flag of truce at half-mast was in reality a national ensign, out of which the mountain rains had washed
every particle of color.   The Stars and Stripes were only
to be distinguished by the seams.   There was comical cause
of mourning ; the bully of Breckenridge — a German gro-
cer — had been whipped, the day before, by the bully of
Buffalo Flats !   The flag-staff is planted in front of a log

court-house. While I was gazing upon the emblem of defeat and regret, I noticed two individuals entering the building. One was middle-aged, and carried a book under his arm; he wore "store clothes." The other, a lively young fellow, with a moustache, sported a flannel shirt. The latter reappeared on the balcony, in a moment, and proclaimed in a loud voice, —

"Oh yes! Oh yes! The Honorable Probate Court is now in session!"

Thereupon he withdrew. The announcement produced no effect, for he immediately came forth again, and cried,—

"Oh yes! Oh yes! The Honorable Probate Court is now adjourned!"

I waited, to see the Honorable Probate Court come forth, with the book under his arm; but, instead of that, the lively young man made his appearance for the third time, with a new announcement, —

"Oh yes! Oh yes! The Honorable Commissioners' Court is now in session!"

How many other Courts were represented by these two individuals, I am unable to say; but the rapidity and ease with which the sessions were held gave me a cheerful impression of the primitive simplicity and peace of the population. To be sure, the flag at half-mast hinted of other customs; yet these may not be incompatible with an idyllic state of society.

We discovered a hotel — or its equivalent — kept by Mr. and Mrs. Silverthorn, who welcomed us like old friends. The walls of their large cabin were covered with newspapers, and presented a variety of advertisements and local news, from New Hampshire to Salt Lake. If the colored lithographs on the wall were doubtful specimens of art, there were good indications of literature on the table. The kind hostess promised us beds, — real beds, with sheets and pillows, — and the good host would have taken me to any number of lodes and gulch-washings, if I had not been

8

almost too sore to bend a joint. I barely succeeded in
going far enough to inspect a patch of timothy grass, grown
from the wild seed of the mountains. It is a slight experi-
ment, but enough to show what may be made of those portions of the Middle Park which are too cold for grain.
The residents of the place profess to be delighted with the
climate, although there is no month in the year without
frost, and the winter snow is frequently three or four feet
in depth. They have very little sickness of any kind, and
recover from wounds or hardships with a rapidity unknown
elsewhere. I was informed that the Honorable Probate
and Commissioners' Court once tumbled down a fearful
precipice, and was picked up a mass of fractures and dis-
locations — yet here he was, good for several sessions a
day!

Our friends, Byers and Sumner, were so chilled to the
marrow by their adventure in the Blue River, that neither
the subsequent ride, nor dinner, nor the hot noonday sun,
could warm their benumbed bodies. They therefore built
a fire in the adjoining wood, and lay beside it nearly all the
afternoon. I would gladly have joined them, but for the
duty of recording our journey, and the task which awaited
me in the evening. The court-house, to my surprise, was
filled with an attentive and intelligent audience, and I regretted that I was unable to comply with their request that
I should recite Mrs. Norton's poem of " Bingen."

There had been some doubt concerning the practicability
of the pass across the main chain to Montgomery, which is
in the South Park, on the head-waters of the South Platte;
but in the afternoon Mr. Matthews arrived, having ridden
from Buckskin Joe to pilot us over. This is called, I believe, the Hoosier Pass; a little to the east of it is the Tarryall Pass, from Hamilton to Breckenridge, which is traversed
by vehicles, even during the winter. There is also a direct
trail from Breckenridge to Georgetown, near the head of
Snake River. Without doubt other and probably better

points for crossing the mountains will be found, when they are more thoroughly explored.

Mrs. Silverthorn kept her promise. When the artist and myself found ourselves stretched out in a broad feather-bed, with something softer than boots under our heads, we lay awake for a long time in delicious rest, unable to sleep from the luxury of knowing what a perfect sleep awaited us. Every jarred bone and bruised muscle claimed its own particular sensation of relief, and I doubted, at last, whether unconsciousness was better than such wide-awake fulness of rest.

I shall always retain a very pleasant recollection of Breckenridge, and shall henceforth associate its name with the loyal divine, not the traitor politician.

XV.

ORO CITY, COLORADO, *July* 4, 1866.

W<small>E</small> deserved no credit for early rising at Breckenridge. The room wherein we slept was also a family-room, dining-room, and parlor, and the ladies of the house could not properly set the breakfast-table in the presence of four gentlemen in shirts. So we issued forth early, to find a white frost on the meadows and a golden glitter of snow all around the brightest of morning skies. Among the Alps, such a morning is a rare godsend; here, it is almost a matter of course. Whatever effect the climate of the Rocky Mountain region may have upon the permanent settlers, there is no doubt that for travellers it is one of the most favorable in the world. It takes fat from the corpulent and gives it to the lean; it strengthens delicate lungs, and paints pallid faces with color; and in spite of "thin air and alkali water," it invigorates every function of the system. I doubt whether any of us, at home, could have ventured on wading in the snow, being ducked in ice-water, and camping on the damp earth with the same impunity.

We still followed up the Blue River, now so diminished that its clear, swift waters had no power to stop our progress. After passing through dilapidated forests of fir and pine for an hour, the trail entered a sloping mountain meadow, several miles long, with a vista of shining peaks at either end. New flowers — turquoise-blue, purple, and yellow — sprinkled the turf; the air was filled with resinous odors, and the sunshine had just sufficient power to take the icy edge off the air and make it fresh and inspiring. The trail, for the most part, was dry and firm, and our travel became something more of a luxury than it had been during the previous days.

Near the head of the valley, immediately under the snowy ridge, there was a great tract which the gold-washers had gone over with unsparing hand. It must have been a rich placer, for two or three inhabited cabins remain, and there were signs of recent labor. The snow-drifts lay thick all around, the grass was just beginning to shoot, and the three-months' summer of the higher ranges, during which only gold-washing can be carried on, had barely made its appearance. The residents were absent (probably prospecting), and there was no living creature to be seen, except a forlorn donkey.

Beyond this spot we came unexpectedly upon the summit of the pass. Our ascent from Breckenridge had been very gradual, and we had not guessed the great elevation of the latter place above the sea-level. This route has been surveyed, and our guide, Mr. Matthews, pointed out the stakes from time to time with great satisfaction. The top of the pass is a little below the timber line, and the stake there is marked " 11,000 feet." The average ascent on the south side is ninety feet to the mile, while the descent on the north only averages seventy feet. The building of a railroad would not be attended with the slightest difficulty. This pass, dividing the Middle from the South Park, is, as I have explained in a former letter, also the water-shed between the Atlantic and Pacific. The grand off-shoots of the main chain of the Rocky Mountains, so numerous and so lofty, are apt to lead the eye astray, and give an impression of difficulties, which disappear on a closer acquaintance with the region. The first entrance of the Pacific Railroad into the mountains will be found, I suspect, quite as difficult as the passage of the dividing ridge.

We halted on the summit, to enjoy the narrow but very striking views into the opposite Parks. Northward, we looked down the long green meadow, with its inclosing slopes of forest, to a line of snow-clad peaks in the middle distance, and then a higher and fainter line, rosily flushed, a hundred miles away — the northern wall of the Park. Southward, the valley of the Platte, a deep gray-green trough, curving out of sight among the lower ranges, bore a striking resemblance to the upper valley of the Saco, as you look upon it from Mount Willard. Beyond it, the increasing dimness of each line of mountains told of broad, invisible plains between; and the farther peaks, scarcely to be detached from the air, were the merest Alpine phantoms. Directly to the west of us, however, rose a knot of tremendous snowy steeps, crowned by a white, unbroken cone. This is Mount Lincoln, believed to be the highest point in Colorado. The estimates vary between fifteen and eighteen thousand feet; but the most trustworthy measurement — which also corresponds with its apparent elevation above the pass — is sixteen thousand six hundred feet. Later in the season, it can be ascended without much difficulty.

It is fortunate that this prominent summit is so appropriately named. It is the central point from which at least four snowy ranges radiate, is one thousand feet higher than any peak which has yet been measured, and the view from its snowy apex can hardly be drawn with a shorter radius than one hundred and fifty miles. Although not standing alone like the volcanic cones of Oregon, but in the midst of a sublime Alpine world, it yet asserts its supremacy, and its huge, wintry buttresses form a prominent feature in the landscapes of the South Park.

We now turned to the right, in order to visit Montgomery, which lies on the very head-waters of the South Platte, at the foot of Mount Lincoln, whose rocky sides are veined with the richest ores. In less than a mile after leaving the top of the pass, we saw the neat little town lying below us, and could detect the signs of mining all around and above it.   I had a surfeit of mining plans and prospects in Central City, and will only say that the people of Montgomery are just as sanguine as those of the former place, and their ores, so far as I could judge from specimens, are just as rich and abundant.   It would interest those who own stock in the North Star, the Pioneer, and other companies, if I should minutely describe their separate lodes; but most of my readers, I presume, will be satisfied with the general statement that the wealth of Colorado has not been, and cannot easily be, exaggerated.

Descending a long and toilsome declivity to the town, we drew up at the post-office.   Friendly hands took charge of our animals, and a dinner was promised in commemoration of our return to the Atlantic side of the Rocky Mountains.   Mr. Valiton, I am glad to say, has become a thorough American in everything but his knowledge of cookery; and the repast he furnished us, although commencing with oyster soup and ending with peaches, bore no resemblance to the dreary fare served up in most of our hotels.   When it was over, and we were enjoying the pipe of peace in the sun, the intelligent company of Mr. Rey, formerly Consul of France at Montevideo, and several American gentlemen, gave an air of refinement and ancient culture to the place. It required an effort to recall the fact that I was in the wildest nook, the very heart, of the Rocky Mountains.

Montgomery, like Breckenridge, is a deserted town.   It once had a population of three thousand, and now numbers three or four hundred.   But as the cabins of those who left speedily became the firewood of those who remained, there are no apparent signs of decay.   On the contrary, the place seems to be growing a little, and as soon as the "new process" is satisfactorily ascertained, it will shoot up into permanent importance.   We had only time to make our nooning there, my place of destination being Buckskin Joe, eight miles further.

We rode five miles down the South Platte, then climbed over one of the many insteps of Mount Lincoln, into a narrower valley, running westward along the base. Near its head, ten thousand feet above the sea, lies the town of the lovely name — a somewhat larger and more active place than Montgomery. The people, for the space of two or three years, made a desperate attempt to change the name to "Laurette," which is slightly better ; but they failed completely, and it will probably be Buckskin Joe to the end of time. At least, it is not a " City " — which, in Colorado, is quite an honorable distinction. There are worse names in California than this, and worse places. If I failed to find a blacksmith, and my barefooted pony must go unshod, we had a carpeted room at the Pacific House, an audience of near a hundred collected in the evening, and everything was done to make my visit comfortable. These remote, outlying mining communities have made a most agreeable impression upon every member of our party. The horde of more or less ignorant adventurers having drifted away to Montana and Idaho, those who remain are for the most part men of education and natural refinement, and their hospitality is a favor in a double sense.

In the evening there was a dismal fall of mingled snow and rain, and I found a fire necessary for comfort. The bare slopes around the village were white for an hour after sunrise. We were here joined by Mr. Thomas, of Chicago, who came from Denver with a mule-team, and brought us late news from the world and letters from home. This morning we took leave of White, who started for Empire with our faithful pack-mules. The latter were a plague at times, with all their service, and we are not sorry to be rid of them ; but I miss White's honest blue eyes.

There are two roads from Buckskin Joe to this place, one practicable only in midsummer for horses, directly over a lofty spur of the snowy range ; the other a rough wagon-trail, which goes down the Platte twelve or fifteen miles before crossing to the Arkansas Valley. Mr. Beard, exulting at his escape from the saddle, took the mule wagon with Mr. Sumner; the rest of us determined to try the shorter and more difficult pass. Mr. Willet, of Buckskin Joe, offered his services as guide, promising to pilot us safely over, although no horses had yet crossed this season. So, wearing the scarlet " Matthews tie," as a memento of that gentleman's kindness, we bade good-by to Buckskin Joe, without visiting the abundant " pay-streaks " in its neighborhood.

One evidence of the richness of the locality met us, how-ever, at the outset. We rode along the borders of a nar row gulch — now all stones and gravel — out of which five hundred thousand dollars were washed in 1860. Thence, two miles over a rough, timbered mountain brought us to Mosquito, another mining village of a hundred inhabitants, at the mouth of a narrow, winding gorge, issuing out of snow-streaked heights to the southward. Into this gorge led the trail, difficult in places, but not to be compared to the swamps and rocky ladders of the Middle Park. Mr. Willet walked briskly in advance, entertaining us with sto-ries of his winter journeys on foot over the pass, carrying the weekly mail. He did not appear to be troubled by the rarity of the atmosphere, of which I was very conscious, even in the saddle.

The ascent was quite gradual, yet we soon passed the timber line, and the fields of snow crept down the steeps of grass and rock, ever nearer, feeding the torrent which rushed through the gorge. On the left towered an appar-ently inaccessible mass of dark-red rock, to the height of two thousand feet; a field of snow in front, shining against the sky, was equally impassable, and the steep on our left must be scaled. We dismounted, and commenced the heart-breaking task. Climbing a dozen steps at a time, and then halting to recover breath, we slowly toiled upward, around a great slant of melting snow, which had lodged under the cornice of the mountain. I could take no note of the wonderful scenery which opened and widened under us, for every pulse throbbed as if ready to burst, my eyes were dim and my head giddy in the endeavor to fill my collapsed lungs. The pony climbed faithfully at my side, and more than once I should have fallen but for his supporting neck.

We circumscaled the snow at last, and came over the sharp crest upon an upland a mile or two long, bounded by the highest summits. It was a bleak, Arctic landscape ; where the snow had melted there were patches of brick-colored rock and brown grass, or pools of dull, chilly water. The great cliffs across the gorge cut off the distant mountains and valleys from view ; we were alone in an upper world as bleak as that on the Norwegian *fjelds*. The summit-ridge we were to cross lay to the southward, but we could detect no way to reach it without crossing broad and apparently dangerous drifts. Mr. Willet, however, who had frequently made the journey in storm and mist, marched on with a confident air, leading us across the table-land, up a stony angle of the mountain, with snow-filled ravines on either side, until we reached a point where it was necessary to dismount for the last climb.

This was the toughest work of all. The trail became a rocky staircase, crossed by drifts thirty or forty feet in depth, where, after walking firmly on the surface for a few yards, man and horse would sink down unexpectedly and flounder in the melting snow. In those lofty regions there is no such thing as getting a " second wind " — every step is like a blow which knocks the breath out of one's body. I was conscious of a dry, disagreeable, tingling sensation in the lungs, which the most rapid, open-mouthed inhalation of air could not allay. At every tenth step we were forced to pause, overcome by what I may call *respiratory fatigue*. The air, nevertheless, was deliciously pure and bracing, and none of us experienced any nausea, bleeding at the nose, or dimness of vision, such as great altitudes

frequently produce. When we stood still, the physical discomfort soon passed away. The ledges of naked red rocks
increased as we climbed; the dark-blue sky sank lower
behind the crest; and at one o'clock in the afternoon we
stood upon the summit of the pass.

Our elevation above the sea-level could not have been
much less than thirteen thousand feet. The timber line
was far below us; near at hand we were surrounded by a
desolation of snow and naked rock. Mount Lincoln, on
the north, gathered together the white folds of the separating mountain ranges, and set his supreme pyramid over
them; while far to the southeast, where the sage-plains of
the South Park stretch for a hundred miles, all features
were lost in a hot purple mist. Before us, however, lay the
crowning grandeur. The ridge upon which we stood slid
down, like the roof of a house, to the valley of the Upper
Arkansas, which we could trace to the very fountain-head
of the river, its pine groves and long meandering lines of
cotton-wood drawn upon a field of pearly gray-green. Starting from Mount Lincoln, the eye followed the central chain
— the backbone of the continent — in a wide semicircle
around the head of the valley until it faced us on the opposite side, and then kept on its course southward, on and
ever on, slowly fading into air — a hundred miles of eter-
nal snow! Beyond the Arkansas Valley (where there is a
pass considerably below the timber line) glimmered, as if
out of blue air, the rosy snow of other and farther ranges.
Westward, seventy miles distant, stood the lonely Sopris
Peak, higher than Mont Blanc.

New landscapes are often best described by comparison
with others that are known; but I know not where to turn
for any mountain view at all resembling this in wondrous
breadth and extent — in the singular combination of sub-
dued coloring with great variety of form. It is at once
simple, sublime, and boundless. With a very clear atmosphere, the effect might be different; as we saw it, the far-

thest peaks and ranges melted insensibly out of the line of vision, suggesting almost incredible distances. There were no glaciers, thrusting down their wedges between the forests; no great upper plateaus of impacted snow, pouring their cataracts from rocky walls, as in the Alps. The snow-line, though broken by ravines, was quite uniform; but the snows were flushed with such exquisite color, and cut the sky with such endless variety of outline, that they substituted a beauty of another and rarer kind. This, and the view of the Blue River Valley, in the Middle Park, are representative landscapes; and they alone are worth a journey across the Plains.

We celebrated the day with none but the most loyal and patriotic sentiments. Our toasts were few, for there was little of the material out of which they grow; our speeches short, for breath was a scarce commodity; but we duly remembered the American Eagle, and magnified the shadow of his wings. There has been no loftier celebration this day in the United States, I am sure.

It was impossible to mount our horses until a certain point, nearly two thousand feet below us, had been reached. There was no snow on the southern slope; but a zigzag, headlong path over bare stones (among which Mr. Byers saw constant indications of gold) for two miles or more, and we reached the bottom with trembling knees and dripping faces. After this the path gradually fell into one of the lateral glens which debouch into the Arkansas Valley, and we pushed merrily on through pine groves and over green meadows, stung by the gadfly of hunger. Mr. Willet insisted on taking us out of the direct path to see the evidences of gold-washing in California Gulch. We objected, preferring to see a dinner; but he was our guide, and he had his way. The obdurate man made us ride along a mile of hideous gravel-pits and piles of dirt, smacking his lips over the hundreds of thousands of dollars which had been dug out of them, while every one of us

was suffering indescribable pangs.   What was it to us that
men are even now washing out one hundred dollars a
day?

Log-cabins made their appearance at last, then miners,
then more log-cabins, then a street with several saloons,
eating-houses, and corrals, — and that was Oro City.   The
place did not promise much, I must confess; but one must
never judge from the outside in Colorado.   What we found
I will relate in my next.

XVI.

SALT WORKS, SOUTH PARK, *July* 6, 1866.

I SAID we were hungry on arriving at Oro City, but the word gives no description of our sensations. After climbing over a crest only a few hundred feet lower than the Swiss Jungfrau, we descended to the level of human life with a profound interest in the signs of " Boarding " and " Miners' Homes," which greeted us on entering the place. Even the " Saloon," with its cubicular bottles of Plantation Bitters, suggested smoked herring and crackers; and these in our condition would have been welcome luxuries. Before we had dismounted, a gentleman of most cheery and hospitable face threw open his door, disclosing arm-chairs and rocking-chairs, a long table, and a dim vision of beds in the background. We entered, and there were presently sounds of dulcet hissing and sizzling in the rear; grateful, but ah! most tantalizing odors in the atmosphere; and then *the trout* were set before us — us, who would have rejoiced over raw pork! It was a meal worth pining for, and I do less than my duty in recording the name of our host, Mr. Wolf Londoner, who not only fed but lodged the whole party, with the most generous disregard of his own and his wife's comfort. I consider that hospitality perfect which does not allow you to feel the sacrifices it imposes; and such was the kind we received in Oro City.

We passed the afternoon in a state of luxurious and commendable idleness. There was no work going on in the gulch, — every one was enjoying the national holiday;

Major De Mary came across the valley with a kind invitation to his ranche and mineral springs, and joined our club of idlers. We not only learned that gulch mining is still profitable in this region, — one company producing one hundred dollars per day per man, — but were presented by our unparalleled host with evidences of the fact, in the shape of nuggets. A lump, found the day before our arrival, weighed three ounces. Promising lodes have been struck, but none are worked as yet.

In the evening one of our party lectured in the Recorder's office, which was draped with flags, and temporarily fitted up as an auditorium. A number of ladies were present, and the new type of face which I have described in a previous letter reappeared again. The question returned to me, — whence is it produced? From the climate of our central regions, the circumstances of life, or the mingling of blood? Possibly a mixture of all three. Whatever it may be, here is the beginning of a splendid race of men. I remembered having been very much puzzled a year ago by the face of a waiter on one of the Mississippi steamers. I fancied I saw both the Irish and the German characteristics, which is such an unusual cross, that I ascertained the man's parentage, and found it to be *Scotch* and German. The Celtic and Saxon elements seem to supply each other's deficiencies, and to improve the American breed of men more than any other mixture. The handsome Colorado type may be partly derived from this source.

After the lecture there was a ball, which all the ladies of the Upper Arkansas Valley — hardly a baker's dozen — attended. The sound of music and dancing, and the assurance that we would be acceptable in our flannel shirts and scarlet " Matthews ties," could not, however, overcome the seductions of Mr. Londoner's beds. To cross the Rocky Mountains two days in succession, speak to the multitude in the evening, and dance afterward, is beyond my powers.

"Fatigue," as Mr. Beard truly remarks, when laying aside a half-finished sketch, "demoralizes." Our host and hostess very properly resolved not to be cheated out of their holiday; and after all the labor our advent had caused, they enjoyed the ball until three in the morning, and then arose at five to make ready for our breakfast.

Our proposed route was down the Arkansas to Cañon City, a distance of a hundred miles, which we hoped to accomplish in three days. The head-waters of the river are at the western foot of Mount Lincoln, the dividing ridge making a horseshoe curve around them. The pass at the head of the Arkansas Valley is probably the lowest between the South Pass and Santa Fé, but on each side of it the ranges rise rapidly above the line of perpetual snow. That on the east, which we had just crossed, is merely a long spur of the Rocky Mountains, dividing the South Park from the Arkansas Valley. It gradually diminishes in height, and finally terminates altogether at Cañon City, where the river issues upon the plains. The range on the west, called the Sahwatch, is at first the dividing ridge of the continent, lifting its serrated crest of snow to the height of fourteen thousand feet. In the course of fifty or sixty miles, however, it divides; the eastern branch uniting with the Sángre de Christo and Raton Mountains, while the western becomes merged in the Sierra Madre of New Mexico, dividing the waters of the Gila from those of the Rio del Norte. The Sahwatch Range is one of the most beautiful of the various divisions of the Rocky Mountains. Its forms are even finer than those seen from Denver. The succession of tints is enchanting, as the eye travels upward from the wonderful sage-gray of the Arkansas bottom, over the misty sea-gray of the slopes of buffalo-grass, the dark purplish green of fir forests, the red of rocky walls, scored with thousand-fold lines of shadow, and rests at last on snows that dazzle with their cool whiteness on the opposite peaks, but stretch into rosy dimness far to the south.

Counting the gradual lower slopes of the mountains on either side, the Arkansas Valley is here five or six miles in breadth ; and you may therefore imagine the splendid morning landscape in pearly shadow, the Sahwatch illuminated from capes of timber, and sage-plains spangled not less with flowers than with dew, as we rode southward toward the Twin Lakes. Major De Mary and Mr. Londoner accompanied us. Our business was first to find Messrs. Beard and Sumner, who had started with the mule-team from Buckskin Joe, and were expected to camp at a deserted ranche eight or ten miles down the valley ; then to accept the invitation of Mr. Leonhardy of the Twin Lakes, and dine with him before proceeding further. On reaching the crossing of the Arkansas, a good field-glass showed us the artist a mile away in pursuit of a mule ; whereupon two gentlemen set off on a gallop to his assistance. The rest of us forded the river, and pushed forward with wet legs down the western bank.

There are very few lakes in Colorado, hence these belong to the shows of the Territory. They lie at the foot of the Sahwatch Range, about fifteen miles south of Oro City. The day was hot and sultry, and we experienced not a little relief when the road, leaving the treeless bed of the valley, mounted to a hilly region covered with clumps of pine. It was miserable to see how many trees had been barked on one side or completely girdled ; and I was on the point of anathematizing the settlers, when one of the party charged the outrage upon the elks. The destruction of this noble game is now a matter of less regret. I don't think, however, that the wanton burning of the Rocky Mountain forests can be attributed to these animals.

Nothing could have been more refreshing than the sudden flash of a sheet of green crystal through an opening in the grove. A cool, delightful wind blew across the water, and far down in its depths we saw the reflected images of snow-peaks which were still hidden from us by the trees.

9

The lower lake is nearly four miles in length by one and a half in breadth, and its softly undulating, quiet shores, form a singular contrast to the rugged mountains beyond. A straight, narrow terrace, twenty feet in height — a natural dam — separates it from the upper lake, which is a mile and a half in length, lying, as it were, between the knees of the mountains. A triangular tract of meadow land slopes upward from the farther end of this lake, and is gradually squeezed into a deep, wild cañon, out of which the lake-stream issues. On this meadow there is the commencement of a town which is called Dayton. The people, with singular perversity, have selected the only spot where a view of the beautiful lake is shut out from them.

Mr. Leonhardy had tempted us with descriptions of six and eight-pound trout; so, when we reached his cottage and were informed by Mrs. L. that he was upon the lake, Mr. Byers, whose love of trout would lead him to fish even in Bitter Creek, at once set off across the meadows. We followed, leaving him to embark in the shaky little craft, while we sought good pasturage for our jaded beasts. The meadow turf was beautifully smooth and green, but before we had ridden twenty yards my pony sunk suddenly to his belly, and I found myself standing a-straddle over him. Looking ahead, I saw Mr. McC. similarly posed over his mule, while the others were making rapid détours to avoid our company. My pony extricated himself by a violent effort, and, taught by instinct, gained safe ground as rapidly as possible; but the mule, being a hybrid, and therefore deficient in moral character, settled on his side, stretched out his neck, and yielded himself to despair. Neither encouragement nor blows produced the least effect; he was an abject fatalist, and nothing but a lariat around his body, with a horse as motive power at the other end, prevailed upon him to stir. The lariat proved efficient. When his hind feet had thus been painfully dragged out of the mire, he pulled out his fore feet and walked away with an air of reproach.

The large specimens of trout did not bite, — they never do when there is a special reason for desiring it, — but we had no right to complain. Mr. Leonhardy's dinner was a thing to be remembered — a banquet, not for the gods, but (much better than that) for men. There came upon my plate a slice of dark fragrant meat, the taste whereof was a new sensation. It was not elk — at least of this earth — nor venison, nor antelope, nor bear, nor beaver ; none of these ever possessed such a rich, succulent, delicate, and yet virile, blood-invigorating flavor. It was mountain sheep — the wild, big-horned American ibex — and to my individual taste it is the finest meat in the world. The trout followed ; and the bread, butter, and milk, could not be surpassed in Switzerland. Lastly came a pudding, stuffed with mountain berries, to crown what already seemed complete. The perfection of the dinner was not in the materials, excellent as they were, but in the refined, cultivated mind which directed their preparation.

The degree of refinement which I have found in the remote mining districts of Colorado has been a great surprise. California, after ten years' settlement, retained a proportion of the rough, original mining element ; but Montana has acted as a social *strainer* to Colorado ; or, rather, as a miner's pan, shaking out a vast deal of dirt and leaving the gold behind. Mr. Leonhardy and his neighbors live in rude cabins, but they do not therefore relinquish the graces of life. It is only the *half*-cultivated who, under such circumstances, relapse toward barbarism. Mountain life soon rubs off the veneering, and we know of what wood men are made.

Some miles up the cañon behind the lakes is Red Mountain, which is said to be streaked through and through with the richest gold and silver lodes. The specimens I saw give the greatest promise, and I regretted that we could not have visited the spot whence they were taken. This region, like the others, is waiting for the best and cheapest

method of reducing the ores.   It is a vast treasure-house,
lacking only the true key to open it.

We took leave of our generous hosts immediately after
dinner, and pushed on down the Arkansas Valley, still
accompanied by Mr. Londoner.   The road led along the
banks of both lakes, close to their deep, dark waters, yet
unsounded ; and over their cool floor the dry, lilac-tinted
mountains in the distance shone as if swept with fire.   We
had received particular directions in regard to fording the
creek by which the lakes overflow into the Arkansas.   It
was so swollen that the usual ford was impracticable ; and,
on reaching its banks, Mr. Byers judged it prudent to
make a platform of drift-wood upon the wagon-bed, in
order to lift our baggage and provisions above the water.
When all was ready for the trial, he remounted his horse
and led the way.

Plunging into an eddy where the water, though above
the horse's belly, was tolerably still, he skirted a little
island of willow bushes, beyond which the main current
raced by with a very perceptible slant, indicating both
depth and force.   We followed in single file, slowly and
cautiously, and did not attempt the current until we saw
that he had fairly reached the opposite bank.   When my
turn came, I fully expected to be carried away.   The water
rushed over the saddle, the horse lost his footing, and
nothing but a plucky heart in the beast carried him through.
Then came the mule-team, Mr. Sumner driving and Mr.
Beard perched upon the platform, with the precious box
of colors in his lap.   I watched them creeping along under
the lee of the island, slowly venturing out into the swift,
strong flood — then the mules began to give way, and presently the whole team started down stream, with one mule
under water.

Mr. Sumner succeeded in getting a little out of the current, and two horsemen went to his assistance.   The wagon
and mules were half urged, half dragged into stiller water,

and there they stuck.   The nose and ears of the drowning
mule were held up by main force; he was unharnessed,
and free to rise.   But he, too, had already given up hope;
he lay passive, and every effort to inspire him to make an
effort was fruitless.   More than half an hour passed anx-
iously, four of the gentlemen working hard in the ice-cold
water, when an application of the lariat, drawn by horses,
brought the wretched beast to his legs.   The baggage was
then carried across, piece by piece, on horseback; the
mule hauled over and contemptuously turned to graze;
another mule harnessed in his place; the lariats made fast
to each other and attached to the wagon-tongue; and
finally, the wet and chilly horsemen crossed, to be ready
to take their places in hauling.   Again the wagon started;
the artist clasped his color-box (and my carpet-bag I grate-
fully add) with renewed energy; the mules entered the
current, wavered again, and were swept away.   Six of us,
pulling at the lariats with all our strength, held the team
and wagon floating for a moment, then the current swung
them to the bank, foothold was gained, and we hauled
them out with a shout of triumph.   The adventure lasted
forty minutes, by the watch.   Those who had been loudest
in their praises of savage nature up to this point, now
began to admit the beauty of bridges.

The summits of the Sahwatch were veiled in clouds, and
the sky became overcast, as we resumed our journey; our
animals were all fatigued and chilled, and our progress for
the next six or eight miles was slow.   My pony had never
been shod, and the hard mountain travel began to tell on
his feet; so when we reached Cache Creek, where there
are three taverns, a store, a saloon, and some gulch mining,
my first inquiry was for the blacksmith.   At Buckskin Joe
I had failed; at Oro the shop had been burned; and now
at Cache Creek the blacksmith, when found, proposed that
I should wait a day.   This was impossible, although three
taverns, a landlord with a bunged eye, and an enterprising

landlady, offered accommodation enough. We had already waited an hour before the blacksmith could be found ; and now, a little dispirited, we set out in a drizzling rain.

A little below Cache Creek the Valley of the Arkansas contracts. The road winds through rocky hills, covered with scattered timber,—sometimes following the river down narrow winding glens, sometimes forced over steep heights to avoid an impassable cañon. We travelled some four or five miles through this scenery, and encamped in a meadow, at the foot of a huge gray precipice. A bonfire of dead pine trunks dried our half-drowned adventurers, and two stately trees made shelter for our beds.

XVII.

CAMP, SOUTH PLATTE RIVER, *July* 8, 1866.

WHEN we encamped on the Arkansas, we were still seventy miles from Cañon City, by the practicable trail. Under ordinary circumstances, this would have been an easy journey, but our animals were fagged by the severe mountain travel, the sky was threatening, our provisions were short, and there was no settlement on the way, except a few miles below us, in the Arkansas Valley. Nevertheless, we determined to push on as far as possible, and, if need be, divide the party at the end of the day.

It was a little hard to come back to the normal diet of salt pork and biscuit, but Mr. Londoner, our faithful ally, set us the example. We slept soundly on elastic mattresses of fir, breakfasted early, and continued our slow way down the valley. There was a deep creek to be forded, and we took the precaution of attaching lariats to the wagon-tongue, whereby a catastrophe like that of the previous day was prevented. After this, the rough, broken country ceased, the valley opened out more broadly, and we saw — or would have seen, but for gathering clouds — the Sahwatch Range. An irrigating ditch from the river pleasantly surprised us. Following it, we came to a large inclosed field of wheat — the first since leaving the neighborhood of Denver. The place is called Frenchman's Ranche from its owner, whom we saw at a distance, engaged in looking after his growing crops. It is a cheerful oasis in the wilderness.

Two miles further we crossed the Arkansas on a rude
but substantial log bridge. The river is here a flashing,
foaming torrent, about the size of the Saco at Conway.
The road, clinging for a mile or two to the grassy meadows
and scattered groves of the valley, gradually climbs along
the hills on its eastern side, and then suddenly enters a
narrow, winding glen. A little further to the south the
great Cañon of the Arkansas, through which no road has
yet been made, commences ; and all the travel from the
farming country below Cañon City to the mining regions
about the head of the river must cross the lower part of
the South Park. Fortunately, the mountain boundaries
of the Park are here broad and low, and the passage of
them is not difficult. Not far from the commencement of
the Arkansas Cañon there is a pass across the Sahwatch
(the " Poncho Pass ") into the great San Luis Park, which
is drained by the Rio del Norte, and extends two hundred
and fifty miles southward into New-Mexico. Governor Gil-
pin says that the San Luis Park is the centre of the Continent — " the best gem upon its zone ".— with a " velvety "
atmosphere, and scenery of a cosmical character.

With the first winding of the glen we entered, the Arkansas Valley disappeared, and the scenery instantly
changed. The hills were heaps of dark red boulders, arranged in fantastic piles — Cyclopean pyramids, sometimes
topped by single blocks, twenty or thirty feet in diameter,
sometimes disposed so as to form apparent bastions in front
of long, tumbling ramparts. Every undulation of the
ranges, far and near, was crowned with these natural ruins.
Out of the thin, sandy soil, grew clumps of *piñones* (a pine
with edible cones), which denoted a warmer climate than
we had yet found in the mountains. The cactus, also, reappeared, and these two features gave a savage picturesqueness to the landscapes.

After a few scorching sun-bursts, the sky became over-
spread with a gray film, gathering into blackness along the

Alpine ranges behind us. For mile after mile we wound through the labyrinths of rocks and bushy pines, a slow, straggling, and rather melancholy procession. My poor, shoeless pony could not be persuaded to trot. Mr. D.'s mule refused to carry him, and he was added to the wagon-load, greatly discouraging its team. Mr. Byers's horse, alone, seemed equal to the emergency. Two of the party pushed ahead, in the hope of finding game, and the remainder of us lagged so much that we were obliged to camp at noon without overtaking them. The rest and pasture slightly encouraged our animals, but it was very evident that we could no longer depend upon them.

We had travelled eight miles after entering the hills, before there were any signs of a " divide." What seemed to be the highest ridge then rose before us. Its crest was bare, and as we emerged from the trees and looked backward, a most remarkable landscape was revealed. Over a foreground of hill-tops, from which shot up hundreds of rocky towers and pyramids, we looked down into the Arkansas Valley, which here formed a basin several miles in breadth. Seen through the filmy atmosphere, the silvery sage-plains seemed to be transparent. The meandering lines of timber which marked the courses of the Arkansas and its tributaries, were of the purest ultramarine hue. In the background, the intensely dark clouds, resting on the summits of the Sahwatch, were lifted in an arch, which was filled with a marvellous glow of pale-gray light, enshrining a great snow-peak in the centre. This was the luminous part of the picture — all else was seen through transparent shadow, the gradations of which were so exquisite, the tones so rare and delicate, that Color itself could scarcely represent them.

We picked up our foiled hunters, whom we found sitting beside a fire, in an attitude of dejection, which may have been the effect of hunger. On the summit of the divide the rain began to fall, though not rapidly enough to obscure the beauty of the long and lovely valley on the other side. As we descended this valley, it soon became evident that we were not yet in the South Park ; it turned westward and slanted toward the Arkansas. Mr. Byers and I held a consultation as we rode, he proposing that we twain should push on for Cañon City, leaving the others (who had no lectures to deliver) to make for Denver. To do this, however, we must take no baggage, and very little provender, ride twenty miles further before camping, and run the risk of my pony giving out on the way. We were on the point of deciding for this plan, when the sky closed over us more darkly than ever, the rain fell in steady, dreary streams, and the road (which, meanwhile, had almost imperceptibly crossed another ridge and entered the South Park) divided into two trails. One of these, Mr. Londoner informed us, led to the Salt Works, about five miles distant, where we could find food and shelter ; the other to Cañon City, with a single deserted ranche on the way.

It was four o'clock in the afternoon : we were hungry, wet, and sore : our horses seemed scarcely able to drag their feet through the mud : the water was slowly soaking through our shoulders and trickling into our boots ; and the heroic resolutions of half an hour previous rapidly melted away as we paused at the parting of the ways. Like many another, the narrow and difficult trail lost its self-denying attractions ; the short and broad trail became suddenly very fascinating. The wind blew and the rain dashed more harshly in our faces ; we yielded, turned our horses' heads, and rode silently toward the Salt Works.

A lone mountain, glimmering dimly across the melancholy plain, was our beacon. Another hour brought to view a column of smoke, rising from its base — the welcome sign of habitation and shelter ! Then we saw grazing herds — white patches of saline incrustations — shanties and cabins, and just before nightfall the goal was reached. The house of Mr. Hall, the superintendent of the works, received our dripping party, so rejoiced to find warmth, food, and protection from the storm, that I am afraid we were not fully aware of the inconvenience we occasioned to our kindly hostess. Ourselves, blankets, saddles, and other traps, almost filled the little cottage; we made a solid circle around the stove; yet, somehow, the bountiful supper was swiftly and quietly prepared, and two strangers who came after us were received with equal hospitality. The life of a settler in Colorado necessarily entails these duties, and if they are always so cheerfully and kindly performed as in our case, the Territory may be proud of its citizens.

Mr. Hall gave me some information concerning the Salt Works, from which it appears that the yield of the springs, which are very strongly impregnated, is capable of supplying the wants of Colorado, for many years to come. In spite of the high price of labor, fuel, and supplies, the production of salt is now vigorously and successfully carried on; the capacity of the works will soon be doubled. I ought, properly, in my character of traveller, to have visited them: the curious reader, perhaps, may not be willing to excuse my neglect; but, at the time, I found it so much more agreeable to nurse my soaked existence beside the stove than to trudge a quarter of a mile in mud and rain, that I suppressed the voice of conscience. We all know, however, that a salt spring is like any other spring, except as to taste; that the water is evaporated by boiling, and that the importance of the works depends on the quantity and quality of the water. I believe Mr. Hall stated twenty thousand gallons per day as the present yield: the percentage of salt is equal to that of the best springs in the world.

That night, we filled the sofas, benches, and the floors of the kitchen and sitting-room. Fir in the trunk, I discovered, makes a much more uneasy bed than fir in the bough.

Toward morning the sleepers were restless, and if we arose before the sun we deserved no special credit for it.   The South Park was still moist, sodden, and shrouded in mist. Cañon City being now out of the question, Colorado City and Pike's Peak were next discussed. Seventy-five miles, partly of very rocky travel, and no blacksmith's shop on the way, were altogether too much for my pony, and we finally decided to make for the little mining village of Fairplay, twenty miles distant, to the north.   Thence to Denver is a three days' journey, along the South Platte. Our animals had enjoyed the richest pasturage during the night, and a lick of salt, so that they were in rather better condition when we started.

This part of the South Park is a nearly level plain, covered with the finest grass.   Detached hills, or short mountain-ridges, some of them streaked with snow, occasionally interrupt the level ; but, looking northward, the view always reaches to Mount Lincoln and the lofty summits of the central chain.   On the eastern and southern sides the mountains are lower, although they rise toward Pike's Peak, which derives its apparent height and imposing appearance from its isolation.   It is separated by a distance of fifty or sixty miles from the snowy spurs of the Rocky Mountains.   The altitude of the South Park is considerably higher than that of the Arkansas Valley : it is, in fact, equal to that of the Middle Park — between eight and nine thousand feet above the sea.   Hence, it is doubtful whether grain can be successfully grown.

Although the mist gathered into clouds, these latter hung low for several hours, hiding the mountains, which constitute the finest feature of the Park scenery.   We passed Buffalo Springs, forded several small affluents of the Platte, vainly tried to plunder an eagle's nest on the top of a pine-tree, and then entered on a slightly undulating plain, eight or ten miles in breadth.   Now, at least, the sky cleared, revealing snowy chains in front and on both sides of us ; stretches of evergreen forests on the lower elevations ; isolated ranges to the eastward — landscapes, shifting in the relation of their forms, but never to be measured with a radius of less than thirty miles. We should have enjoyed the scenery more keenly, but for our anxiety to reach Fairplay. Mr. Byers pointed out the location of the place near the foot of the northern mountains, yet many a weary mile still intervened. The plain terminated in a belt of scattering timber, then dropped down a slope into broad meadows, crossing which we found ourselves on the edge of a bluff, with the main stream of the South Platte foaming fifty feet below us.

The bridge had been washed away, and fording, after our previous experiences, was anything but an agreeable necessity. The water was so very swift that I fully expected to see Mr. Byers carried away ; but it proved not to be deep, and the bottom was firm. Leaving the others to haul the wagon across, I pushed on up the other bank to Fairplay, left my pony with the blacksmith, and engaged dinner for the party in a spacious log hotel, kept by the genial and loyal Judge Castillo. Fairplay is a quiet little place, with perhaps two hundred inhabitants, at the foot of a wooded slope, looking to the south, with a charming view far down the Park. There is gulch-mining along the Platte and its small tributaries, and lodes, I am told, in the adjacent mountains. Although the rains returned in the afternoon and the sky was threatening, we determined to make ten miles more before night.

The road was rolling, and still heavy from the rains, crossing the low spurs and insteps of hills thrust out from the snowy range. We made slow and weary progress, but the latter part of the way was illuminated with a wonderful sunset. Under the glowing orange of a cloud-bank in the east, the mountains around Pike's Peak lay in ashen shadow, and all the broad, intervening plain, rosy-gray, shimmered with faint, evanescent tints of green and turquoise-blue and gold, where the light struck across it.

This was no fleeting effect : it lingered for at least half an
hour, slowly darkening until the contrasts of light and
shade became as weird and unearthly as in some of the
sketches of Doré.   Before the stars appeared, we reached
our destination, " Dan's Ranche," a two-story frame tavern,
kept by a German.   There was a dark, dirty bar-room, in
which half a dozen miners were waiting for supper ; good,
clean beds and bed-rooms, and a landlady who conversed
enthusiastically with me about Schiller.

Four or five miles north of this ranche lies Hamilton,
at the foot of the Tarryall Pass, by which wagons cross the
snowy range to Breckenridge.   The soil, in all this portion
of the Park, shows " color," and the beautiful swells and
undulations which delighted our eyes are destined, no
doubt, to be dug up, washed down, and torn to pieces.
Already hydraulic mining has commenced, and the yield
of the earth is half an ounce a day per man.   This is the
only part of Colorado where I have seen this form of mining applied.   There was a slight attempt at gardening at
the ranche, apparently made without much hope of success,
yet I thought it promised very well.

This morning we awoke to a cloudless sky — every shred
of vapor had disappeared, and the dewy plains glittered in
the sunshine.   We saddled immediately after breakfast,
and set out to cross the northeastern corner of the Park
to the opposite mountains, which were ten or twelve miles
distant.   Had our beasts been fresher, it would have been
an inspiring ride.   The ground was traversed by Fremont
in one of his explorations (I think in 1842 or '43), but
how little he has told us of the scenery !   The idea one gets
from his descriptions and those of other explorers, is that
of dark, stern, *northern* mountains, — the Adirondacks or
White Mountains on a larger scale, — whereas, in color and
atmospheric effects they have all the characteristics of a
southern latitude.   The chain of the Taurus in Asia Minor
most resembles them.   They have nothing in common with
our conventional American scenery.   Bierstadt's large pic-

ture gives a fair representation of some of their forms (though the height of his central peak is exaggerated), but he has not chosen their peculiar atmosphere.

When we had noticed Hamilton at a distance, and the two log-cabins which mark the site of the deserted town of Jefferson; when we had caught sight of Pike's Peak through a long vista between the hills, passed ruined ranches where men were murdered, and meadows of peat which burned under all the winter's snows, — the boundary of the South Park was reached, and we climbed the bare steep, from the summit of which we should look upon it for the last time.

At this point it has the appearance of a little enclosed world, like the Valley of Mexico. The lesser undulations of the soil vanish, but the loftier ridges scattered over its surface and more or less wooded, make dark waves on its broad ground of faint golden-gray. At a distance of twenty or thirty miles the colors appear transparent; still further, the purple peaks, capped with snow, are painted on the air. The most distant tints are pale lilac rather than blue. On the right, the great snowy range carries its grand, solid, positive features beyond the line where the Park becomes more of a vision than a reality, and its sharp rock-shadows and snow-fields keen against the sky form a wonderful contrast to the airy, sunlit gleam of the plains below. On the one hand there is softness, delicate color, and vanishing distance; on the other, height, strength and dazzling clearness.

Yet, as I write, I feel only what my words fail to convey. All the rarer and subtler qualities of the picture fade in the effort to express them. If the characteristic features of Rocky Mountain scenery can be inferred from the fragments of description scattered through these letters, I shall be satisfied. It is impossible to compress them into a single paragraph. Each day's travel, and almost every landscape of each day, has its own distinct individuality.

XVIII.

DENVER, COLORADO, *July* 12, 1866.

WITH the parting view of the South Park we left the chief glories of the Rocky Mountains behind us. The main branch of the South Platte finds an outlet to the plains through a cañon which is yet impassable, and the road to Denver strikes diagonally across the eastern spurs of the snowy range, where the scenery is generally of a rough, cramped, and confined character. For some miles we had very fine views of the lofty peaks at the south-eastern corner of the Middle Park, but after passing the "Kenosha House," a lonely tavern-ranche, the road lay mostly through close, winding dells, leading us to one of the branches of the Platte. Our anglers succeeded in getting a dozen trout, which made a welcome addition to our diminishing stores. We might have found a tolerable "square meal" at the tavern, but our camp-life was drawing near its close just as we were becoming properly habituated to it, and there was no dissenting voice to the proposition that we should avoid both kitchens and roofs for the rest of the journey. A single exception was allowed, toward evening, in the purchase of a loaf of bread.

I have no doubt that, had the course of our journey been reversed — had we been fresh from the monotony of the Plains — we should have found the scenery very delightful. Though the glens were hot, close, and dusty, the road occasionally passed over breezy ridges, whence there were bold views of the lower mountains. We missed the breadth and

sweep of the Parks and the Arkansas Valley, with their
new and wonderful coloring. During the last fortnight the
soil has become parched and dry, and even the narrow
patches of meadow, fed by living springs, have a brownish
hue. The absence of vivid green turf, the scarcity of ferns,
and the lack of variety in the forms of the timber, are
noticeable in this portion of the mountains. It occurs to
me, as I write, that I have not discovered the first specimen of *moss* since reaching Colorado. Even where there
is perpetual moisture, moss is absent; the rock-lichens,
also, are rare. On the other hand, the flora is superb.
We had found but very few flowers in the South Park;
but now the road was fringed with the loveliest larkspurs,
columbines, wild roses of powerful and exquisite odor, gilly-
flowers, lupines, sweet-peas, and coreopsis. The trees were
principally fir, pine, and aspen. A variety of balsam-fir,
with young shoots of a pale-blue tint, grew in moist places.
Those of us who suffered with sunburn or bruises opened
the gummy blisters of the young trees, and anointed ourselves with the balm. In my own case, the effect was
marvellous, — the pain of days was healed in an hour or
two.

We passed two ranches, with their beginnings of agriculture, during the afternoon, and encamped before sunset
in a charming spot on the banks of the stream. Great
towers of rock rose on either side, leaving us barely room
for the beds and camp-fire, beside the roaring water. Up
the Valley we saw mountain forests and a distant snowy
peak. Mr. Beard and I decided that our fir-bed, now much
more skilfully made than at the start, was preferable to
lodging in any hotel in Colorado. We had stories around
the camp-fire that evening; and for the first time during
the trip no one seemed in haste to get under his blankets.

We had not gone a mile down the Valley next morning
before we came upon another camp, much more luxurious
than our own. There was a powerful two-horse wagon, a

10

tent, trunks, and provision boxes. The party which had
thus preëmpted one of the prettiest spots in the Valley
consisted of Mr. Ford, the artist, of Chicago, with his wife,
and Messrs. Gookins and Elkins, also Chicago artists.
They had made the entire trip from the Missouri in the
wagon, and were now on their way into the Parks for the
summer. Mrs. Ford, I was glad to notice, was not the
least satisfied member of the party, though the artists were
delighted with what they had found — and the best was
yet to come. Mr. Whittredge, who crossed the Plains with
General Pope, was at that time in the neighborhood of
Pike's Peak ; so that Art has sent *five* pioneers to the
Rocky Mountains this Summer.

While we were looking over the sketches, the hospitable
mistress of a ranche a little further down the stream made
her appearance, with a basket of eggs for Mrs. Ford. She
could have brought nothing more scarce and valuable —
not even nuggets of gold. We passed a pleasant hour with
the artists, and then left them to push on toward the South
Park, our own hope being to get out of the mountains
before camping.

Leaving this branch of the Platte, we struck across the
line of the ranges, which are here intersected by many lateral valleys. There is a good wagon-road, of a much more
easy grade than that from Denver to Central City. In one
of the glens I met Mr. L., of Philadelphia, who called out,
in passing, — " The President has signed the Railroad
Bill ! " This was good news to the Coloradians of the
party. The Smoky Hill route, on account of its forming
the shortest and most direct connection with St. Louis
and the eastern cities as far as New York, is becoming
more and more popular here, especially since it is uncertain whether the Central Pacific Railroad will touch
Denver.

The day was excessively hot, not only in the glens, but
upon the heights ; and our animals suffered much from the

attacks of flies. We had a journey of more than thirty miles to make ; or nearly ten hours, measuring by the pace of the weary horses. When we halted at noon, the mules ran into a willow thicket and there remained; while my pony left off grazing and came to me, holding down his neck that I might brush away his tormentors. There was so little variation in the scenery that I should only confuse the reader by attempting to describe it in other than general terms. The peaks of the snowy range were seldom visible. It was, apparently, a broken, hilly region, out of which rose wooded ridges or isolated summits, faced with bold escarpments of rock. The soil was thinly covered with grass, gray on the slopes and green in the bottoms ; timber was plentiful but not of large size; yet the few evidences of farming which we met from time to time showed that a great part of the region may be made productive. We passed a number of ranches in the course of the day, in one of which a notable speculation was recently made. A daughter being about to be married, the mother invited the neighbors far and near to the number of forty. They came, supped, danced, and wished good luck to the nuptials, and — were each presented with a bill of six dollars !

As we drew nearer to the Plains, the signs of settlement and travel increased. We passed a saw-mill in operation, a two-story hotel at a place called Junction (whence there is a road to Central City), and many a " preëmpted " tract in the sheltered little valleys. Late in the afternoon we reached Bradford's Hill, Mr. Byers cheering us up the ascent with the assurance that it was the last of the Rocky Mountains. For nearly two miles we toiled along in the scorching sun, sometimes pausing in the thin aspen shade to look backward on some rock-buttressed peak. The summit was wooded, but an opening presently disclosed to our sight a far, blue horizon-line, probably a hundred miles to the eastward. It was only a passing glimpse, and as comforting as water in a thirsty land.

On the first step of the descent, I found for the first
time — *oaks*. They were small saplings, which had sprung
up where the large primitive trees had been felled. Mr.
Byers informed me that he had frequently seen trunks two
feet in diameter, all of which have now disappeared. The
mountain pine is a soft, spongy wood, liable to a great deal
of shrinkage ; the carpenters even declare that it shrinks
" endwise." Cotton-wood is only fit for interior work, so
that good building lumber is scarce, in spite of the abundant forests. I am not surprised that the oaks were swept
away, but I regret that it was necessary.

I have said nothing of the wild fruits of the mountains,
which have become of some importance in the absence of
orchards. The currants, gooseberries, and ·service-berries
(*amelanchier*) are found everywhere ; the bushes are small,
yet bear profusely. Whortleberries are also found, but not
in such quantities. There is a wild red cherry, a plum,
and, in the southern part of the territory, grapes. Strawberries carpet the forests up to the line of snow, but will
not be ripe for two or three weeks to come. They resemble precisely the small, fragrant fruit of Switzerland and
Norway. With the exception of the " Oregon grape " (*mahonia*), I noticed no new varieties of fruit. The cones of
the *piñones* appear to be the only edible nuts. There is a
singular poverty in the Rocky Mountain *sylva*.

While we were discussing the matter of oaks, the road
climbed a little ridge, turned around a bare, stony headland, and — there ! Half a continent seemed to lie beneath
us. We stood on the eaves of the mountains, above all
the soil between us and the Atlantic Ocean. As from the
car of a balloon, or the poise of a bird in mid-air, we looked
down on an immense hemisphere of plain, stretching so
far that we could only guess at its line of union with the
sky. North, south, and east, the vision easily reached a
hundred miles. Wild plain, farm-land, and river-courses
were as distinctly marked and colored as on a map. We

saw the South Platte, issuing from its mountain gateway, gathering Plum, Cherry, and Bear Creeks, skirting Denver, and curving far away on its course toward Julesburg and Nebraska. Beyond Denver, the valleys of Clear Creek, Boulder, Thompson, and St. Vrains were distinctly marked, and somewhere in the vapors of the horizon lay Cache-la-Poudre. Scarcely a house or a tree in all this vast landscape was hidden from view. Its uniform tint of dead gold contrasted exquisitely with the soft blue-gray and pink-flushed snows of Long's Peak and his neighboring summits in the north.

Looking at the base of the mountains immediately below us, I became aware of a remarkable feature of their structure. Parallel with the general direction of their bases, and from a quarter to half a mile distant, ran a straight outcropping of vertical rock, abruptly broken through by the streams which issued upon the plains. Each section of this ridge, which was from one to two hundred feet in height, resembled a ship's hull, keel upward. They are called "hog's-backs" in Colorado. Not only is their formation distinct from that of the mountains, but they are composed of different rock — mostly limestone, gypsum, or alabaster. Their peculiar appearance suggests the idea of their having been forced up by the *settling back* of the great chain of the Rocky Mountains, after upheaval. I am told that this formation extends for a long distance along the eastern base of the mountains.

As the road wound back and forth down the bare, treeless slope, contracting the semicircle of the plains, the objects enclosed within this lower rampart attracted us more and more. Much of the space near at hand was already farmed, and green with lush fields of wheat, and the narrow terrace which it formed, seemed, at first sight, to have been inhabited for thousands of years. What appeared to be the ruins of giant cities arose behind the walls of rock, casting their shadows across the green. Rude natural towers, obelisks, and pyramids, monoliths two hundred feet in height, of a rich red color, were gathered in strange labyrinthine groups, suggesting arrangement or design. Beyond the Platte there was a collection of several hundred of these.· Mr. Byers, who had visited the place, assured me that they greatly surpass the curious rock-images near Colorado City, called the " Garden of the Gods." A nearer view of them through a glass filled me with astonishment. I saw single rocks a hundred feet square, and nearly as high as Trinity spire, worn into the most fantastic outlines, and in such numbers that days might be spent in examining them. On our own road there were several detached specimens of lesser height, and beyond Bear Creek two lofty masses of a rude Gothic character. The wonders of Colorado have not yet been half explored, much less painted.

Our proposed camping-place lay inside the nearest " hog-back," at the foot of one of those rocky masses. We came down the long slant and reached the spot before sunset, less fatigued by the journey than by the great labor (both of spirit and flesh) of keeping up the failing courage of our animals. Our bread was at an end, but Colonel Bradford's ranche, with its stately stone residence, seemed to offer indefinite supplies; so, after unsaddling beside the rock and turning the beasts loose to graze, we called upon the Colonel in a body. He kindly gave us all he had — not bread, but flour and soda, a bunch of onions from the garden, and a wash-basin full of lettuce. Moreover, we had unlimited water from a spring in the garden, and milk from the dairy. The Colonel, a native of Alabama, is justly proud of his ranche, the location of which is wonderfully picturesque.

Mr. Sumner and I made slapjacks of the flour, and with a little exertion we got up a passable meal at twilight. Our beds were soon made among the fragrant herbs, and the night passed rapidly and quietly, except that a coyote stole the remainder of our pork. The breakfast, however, was a matter of little consequence, as we expected to dine in Denver. A fierce African sun came up in the cloudless sky, driving away in ten minutes the scanty dew that had fallen. After more coffee and slapjacks we packed hastily and started on the last pull of sixteen miles. Four of the gentlemen determined to go up Bear Creek and fish for trout; Messrs. Beard and Thomas, with the mule-team, and I on my pony, made a direct line for civilization.

By the time we reached Bear Creek crossing, the heat was intense. My pony had at last reached the limit of his performance, and I was fain to dismount, seat myself in the rear of the wagon, and pull him after us with the lariat. We resisted the shady invitation of the "Pennsylvania Hotel" beside the stream, admired as much as was possible in our condition the splendid fields of wheat, farm succeeding to farm from the mountains to the Platte, and then took to the rolling, fiery upland. Two hours more, and from a ridge we hailed Denver, only three miles away, its brick blocks flashing in the sun, its square spire shooting above the dark green cotton-woods, and its shallow river reflecting the blue of the zenith — a consoling sight!

What life there was in the mules, had to come out then: we all became suddenly conscious that we were dirty, ragged, hungry, thirsty, and terribly fatigued. An intense longing for the comforts and conveniences of life moved our souls: Denver became to us what New York is to the moral native of Connecticut. I am not ashamed to confess that we halted at the lager-beer brewery, half a mile from the town, and took a refreshing draught to correct the effects of the "thin air and alkali water."

The Platte bridge was crossed and we entered the streets, a party more picturesque than respectable in appearance. There were three battered wide-awakes; three flannel shirts, one scarlet, one blue, and one gray; three brown faces, one skinless nose, and one purple ditto. ; dusty rolls of blankets, a bent coffee-pot, a box of colors, and some saddles.   This was the picture which slowly moved up Laramie and F Streets, and stopped at the door of the Pacific Hotel.

XIX.

A TRIP TO BOULDER VALLEY.

DENVER, COLORADO, *July* 14, 1866.

MY days in Colorado are drawing rapidly to an end. The term of the summer holiday which I have allowed myself is nearly over; yet while I have every reason to be satisfied with what has been seen and done in a brief space of time, I find myself regretting, at the close, that I am not able to make my survey of the territory more complete.

The change from camp-life in the mountains to the comparative luxury of a hotel in Denver, was so very agreeable that for two days I did little else than enjoy it, and complete my lost knowledge of the world's doings, up to the point of comprehending the telegrams of national and foreign news. The weather was almost insupportably hot during the day — 98° in the shade — and the better part of one's life was expended from eight o'clock in the morning until sunset, in a vain effort to be cool. Every afternoon a lurid mass of clouds gathered along the sunny range, distant thunders echoed among the peaks, lightnings dashed feebly through the shadows, and the storm dissolved again. We were just near enough to gasp in its sultriness, without catching a drop of its refreshment.

Before setting out on my mountain trip, I had made an engagement to visit the Boulder Valley, twenty-five miles to the north of Denver. Yesterday was the appointed day, and when the morning came with a burning, breathless heat, I lamented, — for a moment, only, — the necessity of the journey. It was the usual shudder before the

plunge.   My faithful pony had been sent back to his pas-
tures in the Middle Park, and I took a saddle-horse at five
dollars per day, at a livery-stable.   I had the owner's word
that he was a good animal ; but the result proved, for the
hundredth time, a truth which I long ago discovered —
that all men who have much to do with horses become demoralized.   Mr. Thomas, of the " Chicago Tribune," had
agreed to accompany me, so that I was sure, at least, of
cheerful society on the way.

We rode out of Denver by the Salt Lake stage road,
which runs northward, parallel with the mountains, for near
a hundred miles.   In the morning air, the snowy peaks,
from Pike's to far beyond Long's, were free from clouds,
and I was struck with the great diminution of snow upon
their sides, since I first saw them.   At the same rate of
melting they will be almost entirely bare in another month.
I doubt whether the line of *perpetual* snow can here be
placed lower than thirteen thousand feet : in the Alps it is
not more than eight thousand.   Their forms were no less
imposing, after seeing the grand landscapes of the Parks,
and there was a constant refreshment in turning from the
heated shimmer of the Plains to the sight of their gorges
in cool shadow, the dark, cloudy patches of their pine forests, and even the bare outlines of their rocky pinnacles,
suggesting tempered sunshine and the breezes of the upper
sky.

In four miles we reached Clear Creek, at a point above
Captain Sopris's ranche.   The stream was so swollen by
the melting snows, that half the bottom was overflowed,
and we rode for a furlong in water up to the horses' bellies.
Irrigation seemed unnecessary ; but the cultivated land is
a mile or more in breadth, and we found the outer ditches
full.   The wheat is in head, and finer crops I never saw,
except in California.   We passed no field which will produce less than thirty bushels to the acre.   It is now considered secure beyond damage from smut or grasshoppers.

The sight of such splendid and bounteous agriculture, here, in the very heart of the continent, is inexpressibly cheering.

The roads leading into Denver from the east, and out of it toward the west, north, and south, now begin to be populous with the usual summer emigration. A considerable number of wagons bring settlers to the Territory — though less than there would be, were its climate and resources generally understood; large freight trains are on their way to Salt Lake (which I hear has become an important business centre, with a population of twenty-five thousand): and many emigrants, bound for Montana and Idaho, have been obliged to make a détour of two hundred miles, through Denver, in order to get over the swollen Platte. One meets, every day, the same variety of characters — the lazy, shiftless emigrant, always trying new countries and prospering in none; the sharp, keen, enterprising emigrant, who would do fairly anywhere, and will rise very rapidly here; the shabby-genteel adventurer, on the look-out for chances of speculation or office; and the brutal, ignorant adventurer, who, some morning, will leave the country "up a tree." The "Rocky Mountain News" will then chronicle the fact in a paragraph headed: "And he went."

The white wagon-covers of some of these parties contribute to the popular literature of the Plains. Many of them are inscribed with the emigrant's name, home, and destination, "accompanied" (as the applicants for autographs say) "with a sentiment." I noticed one which was simply entitled "The Sensible Child." Another had this mysterious sentence, which I will not undertake to explain: "Cold Cuts and Pickled Eel's Feet." "The Red Bull," and "Mind Your Business," were equally suggestive; but the most thrilling wagon-cover was that which met our eyes on crossing the Platte Bridge, and whereon we read: "Hell-Roaring Bill, from Bitter Creek!" In the shade of the cover, between the wheels, Hell-Roaring Bill himself was resting. He looked upon us with a mild, sleepy eye ; his face and breast were dyed by the sun to almost the exact color of his hair ; his general appearance was peculiar, but not alarming. When we returned this morning he had departed, and, if all they say of Bitter Creek be true, I think he has done well in changing his residence.

After leaving the wheat fields of Clear Creek, we rose again to the " second bottoms," or *rolling* table-land (this sounds like a bull, but it describes the thing), where the crimson and golden blossoms of the cactus burned in the intense sunshine, all over the scorched, cracked soil. Thus we rode over the tawny, treeless swells, for seven or eight miles, in a suffocating heat. We then left the stage road, and took a trail leading to the iron and coal mines of Belmont, at the base of the mountains. The thunder-storm was already collecting in the southward, and drew toward us, following the range and blotting out peak after peak in its course. Presently the clear, cool shadows crept down from the upper heights, quenching the fiery red glare of the masses of rock, two thousand feet in height, before us ; then it touched the Plains, crept nearer to us, and the sting of the sun was withdrawn.

The local limits of these storms was very strikingly marked. At the distance of a few miles from the mountains the clouds ceased to spread. Though behind us they gloomed like night, and under their grand, majestic arch we looked into distant floods of rain and lightning, the eastern half of the sky remained cloudless, and the Plains, for leagues away, smouldered in fiercest heat. The rain, also, seemed to be confined to a second limit, inside the line of cloud. The great irregular pyramid of Long's Peak, full in front of us, became a shadow on the air ; the vast nearer piles of red rock were silvered with slanting sheets, and we expected, every moment, to feel the drops. But the sheets moved on, northward, as if with half-spread wings : we only touched their outer edge, on reaching Belmont, and that, because we rode toward them.

This is a charming little valley, at the base of the mountains. The outcropping of limestone, and the black piles at the mouths of coal drifts indicated our approach to it. On dropping into a little winding hollow, we soon saw the massive smelting furnace surrounded by clustered cabins. Mr. Marshall, the proprietor, received us at the door of his residence, and, after dinner, piloted us to the furnace and mines. There are *eleven* veins of coal, varying from four to twelve feet in thickness, in the space of half a mile ; iron ore of a richness of fifty per cent. just beyond it, and the best limestone, in almost inexhaustible quantities. Mr. Marshall, however, has only experimented with the native ores sufficiently to establish their value. He finds it more profitable to buy up abandoned machinery at a trifling cost, and recast it. The furnace is not only substantially but handsomely built, and has thus far done a thriving and successful business for its owner.

Our inspection of the place was necessarily hurried, as I had an engagement for the evening at the new town of Valmont, some eight or ten miles down the Boulder Valley. I looked longingly toward the magnificent gorge by which the South Boulder issues from the mountains, and the sheltered semi-basin beyond, where we saw the town of Boulder above the cotton-woods ; but there was not time (without better horses) to extend our journey so far. The extent and beauty of the cultivated land watered by the two streams, was a new surprise. For miles farm followed farm in uninterrupted succession, the breadths of wheat, black-green in its richness, or overrun with a yellowing gleam, dotted with houses and clumps of trees, like some fenceless harvest-plain of Europe ! A spur of softly-tinted hills in the north, the solitary, rock-crowned hill of Valmont in the east, the snows of Long's Peak to the northwest — these were the features enframing the lovely valley. Here I saw again how much Civilization improves Nature.

We were full two hours in reaching Valmont, on account of the very independent habits of the Colorado farmers. The second bottoms being devoted to grazing purposes, they have found it necessary to fence the outer edge of the farm land; and, in so doing, they cut off the road with the most utter disregard of the public. If there are laws in relation to roads, they seem to be a dead letter. That which should be the first business of a territorial government, is left to a time when it can only be regulated by a great deal of trouble and expense. Our National Government acts in the most niggardly manner toward its incipient States. There should be at least a million of dollars annually spent in each Territory between the Mississippi and the Pacific, on roads and bridges.

In spite of the tedious zigzags we were forced to make, the views of the broad, prosperous, and thickly-settled Boulder region, made our ride very enjoyable. On approaching the isolated hill which had been pointed out to us as indicating the position of Valmont, we were surprised to find no sign of a village. The dark wheat-plains swept up to its base, masses of rock looked down from its summit, and the rosy ridges toward St. Vrains lay beyond. We turned a corner where the fields had almost forced the road off the level, and there stood perhaps a dozen new cabins, and a few scattering cotton-woods. But of these cabins one was a store, one a printing-office, and one a Presbyterian church. So it was Valmont.

We found comfortable quarters at the house of Mr. Jones, a farmer, who has been on the spot six or seven years, and has made himself a pleasant home. After supper, the other farmers began to arrive from up and down the stream, and even from St. Vrains — shrewd, intelligent men, every one of them, and with an air of health and vigor which speaks well for the climate. I would have much preferred talking with them all the evening to lecturing in the church. I wondered, on arriving, where an audience was to come from, and was not a little astonished to find more than a hundred persons gathered together. What I had looked upon as a task became a pleasure, and the evening I spent at Valmont was one of my pleasantest in Colorado.

The people informed me that the farming on the St. Vrains is fully equal to what I saw on the Boulder — that the valleys of the Big and Little Thompson, and even of the Cache-la-Poudre, are settled and cultivated, and will this year produce splendid crops. The line of settlement is thus not only creeping northward and southward from Denver, but, also, following the tributaries of the Platte, it advances eastward to meet the great tide approaching it. I verily believe that it will not be more than two or three years before there is a continuous belt of settlement — probably two of them — from the Missouri to the Rocky Mountains.

I was introduced to one of the original eight squatters in Boulder Valley. He tells a singular story of their experience with the Indians, when they first settled here, in 1859. Where the town of Boulder now is, was one of the favorite camping-grounds of the former. They not only warned the intruders away, but threatened to exterminate them if they remained. The eight men, however, constructed a rude fort, and made preparations to stand a siege. Hostilities commenced and were carried on for some time, when, one day, the besieged noticed signs of commotion in the Indian camp. Toward evening a warrior arrived, demanding a parley. They hesitated for a while, but finally admitted him, whereupon he stated that the medicine-man of the tribe had dreamed, the night before, of stars falling from heaven and a flood from the mountains sweeping away their camp. This he interpreted as a warning that they should leave, and the tribe, therefore, were preparing to depart. The next morning they packed their tents, and after uttering in concert a mighty howl of lamentation, went out on the Plains, and never afterward returned.

We started early this morning, to avoid the terrific mid-day heats. For our entertainment and that of our horses, at Valmont, we were only asked to pay two dollars and a half each. The farms were lovelier than ever in the fresh morning light, and as we paused on a ridge to take a last look at the place, we pronounced it the prettiest village-site in Colorado. Then came the open, unsheltered, rolling Plains, gathering heat and dryness from hour to hour. Toward noon the inevitable storm crept along the mountains, but we were outside of its shadow, under the burning half of the sky — and long indeed were the last few miles which brought us into Denver. My face still burns with the blistering heat absorbed during the ride ; but I rejoice that I have seen Boulder Valley before leaving the Rocky Mountains.

XX.

COLORADO AS A SUMMER RESORT.

DENVER, COLORADO, *July* 15, 1866.

THIS is my last night in Denver. After a month beside and among the Rocky Mountains, I am going (as the people here say) "to America." My place is taken in the stage which leaves to-morrow morning for the East, by the Platte route.

Had not the commencement of the rainy season and the condition of our animals prevented me from reaching Cañon and Colorado cities, my tour would have embraced all of the mountain regions which are easily accessible, and some that are not so. What I have seen is amply sufficient to convince me how much more there is to see. During a journey on horseback of four hundred miles, which led me through two of the three Parks, and thrice across the great range, I have obtained a tolerably extensive knowledge of the climate, scenery, and other features of a region which is destined, I think, to become for us what Switzerland is to Europe. Our artists, with true instinct, have first scented this fact, and they are the pioneers who point out to ignorant Fashion the way it should go.

Whoever comes to the Rocky Mountains with pictures of the Alps in his memory, expecting to find them repeated on a grander and wilder scale, will certainly be disappointed. He will find no upper world of unbroken snow, as in the Bernese Oberland; no glaciers, thrusting far down between the forests their ever-moving fronts of ice; no con-

11

trast of rich and splendid vegetation in the valleys; no flashing waterfalls; no slopes of bright green pasturage; no moss; and but rarely the gleam of lakes and rivers, seen from above. With no less lofty chain can the Rocky Mountains be measured, it is true; but it is merely a general comparison of height, not of resemblance in any important feature.

In the first place, the atmospheric effects are those which result from the intense dryness of the heart of a continent in the temperate zone. The Alps not only touch the Mediterranean at either extremity, but are no further from the Atlantic than from here to the Missouri River. Four or five cloudless days in succession are considered a rare good fortune by the tourist; the higher peaks are seldom without their drapery of shifting cloud. Here a clear sky is the rule. There is seldom vapor enough — except just at present, during the brief rainy season — for the artist's needs. Perspective is only obtained by immense distances. The wonderful, delicate grays of the mountain landscapes demand changes of light and shadow which are often lacking; they lie too barely in the broad, unobstructed sunshine. Yet an air more delicious to breathe can scarcely be found anywhere. It is neither too sedative nor too exciting; but has that pure, sweet, flexible quality which seems to support all one's happiest and healthiest moods. Moreover, it holds in solution an exquisite variety of odors. Whether the resin of the coniferous trees, the balm of the sage-bush, or the breath of the orchis and wild rose, it is equally grateful and life-giving. After a day in this atmosphere you have the lightest and most restorative slumber you ever knew.

On first entering the Rocky Mountains, you find the scenery rugged, cramped, and somewhat monotonous. Press forward, and they open anon — the higher the summits become the more breadth of base, the clearer outline they demand. They push away the crowd of lower ridges, leaving valleys for the streams, parks with every variety of feature, and finally gather into well-defined ranges, or spurs of ranges, giving you still broader and grander land-scapes.

The San Luis Park, from the accounts I have heard, must be equally remarkable. It is on a much grander scale, and has the advantage of a milder climate, from its lesser elevation above the sea-level. The North Park is rarely visited except by an occasional prospecter or trap-per. It has no settlement, as yet, and I have met with no one who has thoroughly explored it. There are a number of smaller parks on both sides of the main chain, and some of them are said to possess great natural beauties. The singular rock formations at the eastern base of the mountains furnish in themselves a rare and most original field for the tourist and the artist. The glimpse I had of those on the south bank of the Platte, on my return from the South Park, satisfy me that they surpass in magnitude and picturesque distortion the celebrated basaltic forma-tions of Saxony.

It was part of my plan to have ascended either Pike's or Long's Peak, but I find that it is too soon in the season to make the attempt. Pike's Peak is comparatively easy of ascent; the summit, thirteen thousand two hundred feet above the level of the sea, has several times been reached by ladies. It is a very laborious, but in no sense a danger-ous undertaking. On account of its isolated position, the view from the top, in favorable weather, must be one of the finest panoramas in the world. Long's Peak has never yet been ascended. Mr. Byers, two years ago, reached a point about five hundred feet below the summit, and was then compelled to return. He is quite confident, however, that it can be scaled from another side, and if the summer were six weeks further advanced, I should be willing to join him in making the attempt. On the northern side he says there is a valley or rather gulf, with walls of perpendicular rock between two and three thousand feet in height, resembling a section of the Yosemite.

A comparison of this peak with Mont Blanc — the altitude of both being just about the same — may give a clear idea of the differences between the Alps and the Rocky Mountains. When you see Mont Blanc from the western part of Lake Leman, in July or August, he appears to you as a dome of complete snow, the few rocky pinnacles which pierce his mantle being hardly discernible specks. He is a *white* vision on the horizon. Long's Peak, at the same distance, is of the faint blue or purple which a rocky mass assumes, veined and streaked with white, but showing only one snow-field of much apparent extent. His outline is very fine, — a little sharper than Mont Blanc, — the western side (as seen from Denver) having convex, and the eastern principally concave curves. He rests on a dark, broad base of forest and rock, his snows marking the courses of deep clefts and ravines. At present, the topmost summit is bare on the southern side. It is rare that one sees Mont Blanc from summit to base : I have not yet seen Long's Peak (except during a passing thundershower) otherwise.

I do not think the parks and the upper valleys of the mountains will produce anything except hardy vegetables, and perhaps barley and rye. But they abound with the richest grasses ; and " Colorado cheese " may one day be as celebrated as Gruyère or Neufchatel. They offer precisely those things which the summer tourist seeks — pure air, lovely nights, the finest milk, butter, trout, and game, and a variety of mineral springs. The summer climate I know ; and I am told that the winter is equally enjoyable. It sounds almost incredible to hear of persons in the latitude of New York, and eight thousand feet above the sea, rarely needing an overcoat during the whole winter season. There is a great depth of snow, and an occasional severe day, but the skies are generally cloudless, and the air temperate and bracing. The extremes of heat and cold are greater in Denver than in the mountains. As nearly as 1 can learn, the coldest weather yet experienced in San Luis Park, was seven degrees below zero; in the Middle Park, fifteen degrees; and in Denver, thirty degrees below.

The heavy snow-fall, while it is a godsend to the agriculture of Colorado, by swelling all the streams at the very season when water is needed for irrigation, nevertheless interferes with the mining interests. There are many rich placers in the mountains where gold-washing can only be carried on for three or four months in the year, and even the stamp and smelting mills are hindered in procuring their supplies. It will also be the principal difficulty which the Pacific Railroad will be obliged to overcome. All other obstacles are much less than I had imagined. Greater achievements have already been done in railroading than the passage of the Rocky Mountains. By the Clear Creek, the South Park, or the Arkansas Valley, the Pacific slope can be reached, with not much more labor than you find on the Baltimore and Ohio road between Piedmont and Grafton. The facilities of construction *beyond* the range, however, must determine where the range should be crossed. A thorough exploration of the region watered by the Green and Blue Rivers must first be made.

I am, therefore, quite unable to tell you where the road will cross the Rocky Mountains; it is enough that they will be crossed. My conjectures — given for what they may be worth — take this form: that the Central Pacific Railroad, now rapidly advancing up the Platte, will cross in the neighborhood of Bridger's Pass; that the Eastern Division will follow the Smoky Hill, and make directly for Denver; that a road running northward along the base of the mountains will connect the two; that this road will then be extended to Montana on one side and New Mexico on the other; and that, finally, a second central road will be pushed westward from Denver into and across the Middle Park, and so to Nevada. The business of Colorado alone, with the stimulus which a completed road would give, will keep that road fully employed. By the time the last rail is spiked down on the road connecting New York and San Francisco, we shall want, not one line across the continent, but *five*.

I hazard nothing, at least, in predicting that Colorado will soon be recognized as our Switzerland. The enervated luxury, the ignorant and imitative wealth, and the overtasked business of our cities, will come hither, in all future summers, for health, and rest, and recreation. Where Kit Carson chased Arapahoes, and Frémont's men ate mule-meat, and Jim Beckworth went through apocryphal adventures, there will be drawling dandies, maidens both fast and slow, ungrammatical mammas, and the heaviest of fathers. The better sort of people will come first, nor be scared away afterward by the rush of the unappreciating. We shall, I hope, have Alpine clubs, intelligent guides, good roads, bridges, and access to a thousand wonders yet unknown. It will be a national blessing when this region is opened to general travel. That time is not now distant. Before the close of 1868 Denver will only be four days from New York, and you can go through with one change of cars. Therefore I am doubly glad that I have come *now*, while there are still buffaloes and danger of Indians on the Plains, camp-fires to build in the mountains, rivers to swim, and landscapes to enjoy which have never yet been described.

The weather continues intensely hot by day, with cool and perfect nights. Sometimes the edge of the regular afternoon thunder-storm overlaps Denver, and lays the hot dust of the streets. These storms are superb aërial pictures. After they pass, their cloudy ruins become the material out of which the setting sun constructs unimaginable splendors. If I were to give the details of them it would seem like color run mad.   Such cool rose-gray, such transparent gold, such purple velvet as are worn by the mountains and clouds, are fresh wonders to me every evening.   The vault of heaven seems ampler than elsewhere; the lines of cloud cover vaster distances, — probably because a hundred miles of mountains give you a more palpable measure of their extent, — and your eye recognizes infinite shades, gradations, and transitions either unseen before or unnoticed.   This amplification of the sky and sky-effects struck me when I first entered upon the Plains.   It is grand, even there; but here, with such accessories, it is truly sublime.

I do not now wonder at the attachment of the inhabitants of the territory for their home.   These mountains and this atmosphere insensibly become a portion of their lives.   I foresee that they will henceforth be among the clearest and most vivid episodes of mine.

XXI.

OMAHA, NEBRASKA, *July* 21, 1866.

ON Monday morning last, Mr. Beard and I took our seats in the overland coach, at Denver. Our hopes of a comfortable trip were blasted at the outset: there were seven passengers for Fort Kearney, and four for the "Junction," as it is called, on the Platte. The fare of one hundred and twenty-five dollars which one pays the Holladay Company, is simply for transportation: it includes neither space nor convenience, much less comfort. The coaches are built on the presumption that the American people are lean and of diminutive stature — a mistake at which we should wonder the more, were it not that many of our railroad companies suffer under the same delusion. With a fiery sky overhead, clouds of fine dust rising from beneath, and a prospect of buffalo-gnats and mosquitoes awaiting us, we turned our faces toward "America" in no very cheerful mood.

The adieus to kind friends were spoken, the mail-bags and way-bill were delivered to the coachman, the whip cracked as a sign that our journey of six hundred miles had commenced, and our six horses soon whirled us past the last house of Denver. The programme of the journey was as follows: across the Plains in an east-by-northern course to the Platte, eighty-five miles; thence to Julesburg, on the line between Colorado and Nebraska, one hundred and fifteen miles more; thence, still following the Platte, to Fort Kearney, two hundred miles more; thence to the western end of the Central Pacific Railroad, wherever we might find it. The agent of the Overland Mail Company in Denver was unable to give me any information upon this latter point. There were rumors that the trains had reached Columbus, one hundred miles west of Omaha, and we preferred to believe them, as they made our anticipations of stage travel less formidable.

It was eight o'clock when we started, and with every hour the heat and dust increased. The long range of the Rocky Mountains, to which we fondly looked back, no longer refreshed us with their distant appearance of coolness ; they might rather be compared to enamelled pictures of pale violet, slowly fixing their colors in a furnace of quivering heat. The green of the Plains was rapidly drying into a tawny hue, and only the cactus, with its splendid flowers, seemed to rejoice in the season. The long swells, extending north and south, between the tributaries of the Platte, gave some little variety to the road. In the hollows the presence of dark-foliaged cotton-woods told of subterranean moisture, although the creek beds showed only dry, hot gravel. The horses were changed at intervals of eight or ten miles, and, when we had made four stations, I was agreeably surprised on our halting for dinner at a neat frame cottage, with stable and post-office adjoining. The meal, at one dollar and fifty cents, was excellent, the water alone having a suspicious flavor of alkali. We made use of a corrective which I would recommend to all travellers — two or three lemons cut into pieces which can be stuffed into a bottle, which fill with good whiskey.

In the afternoon, when the breathless heat and fine, suffocating dust were scarcely to be endured, there came a merciful relief. The mountain thunder-storm either took a wider sweep than usual, or varied from its course at the head-waters of Cherry Creek, and came down the divides toward us. The cool shadows crept over the landscape, and after a time the rain followed. Then ensued a new

annoyance : our outside passengers came in, and ten large
persons must occupy the space designed for nine dwarfs.
Toward evening the clouds lifted for an hour or two, and
we took our last look at the Mountains, lying dark and low
on the horizon. The passengers for the Junction were
pleasant fellows, and I mean no disrespect in saying that
their room was better than their company. After sunset
another setting in of rain drove them upon us, and by
eleven at night (when we reached their destination) we
were all so cramped and benumbed, that I found myself
wondering which of the legs under my eyes were going to
get out of the coach. I took it for granted that the nearest pair that remained belonged to myself.

The artist and I had now possession of the back seat;
but our condition was not greatly improved. We tried
various devices with rolls of blankets, but all to no purpose. The coach is so ingeniously constructed that there
are no *corners* to receive one's head. There is, it is true,
an illusive semblance of a corner ; if you trust yourself to
it, you are likely to lean out with your arm on the hind
wheel. Nodding, shifting of tortured joints, and an occasional groan, made up the night. There was no moon, and
nothing was visible except the dark circle of the Plains
against the sky.

At four o'clock in the morning, as the daylight was
creeping up under the clouds, we halted at a singular station. A wall of adobes three feet thick and six in height,
pierced with loop-holes for musketry, confronted us. The
top was rudely machicolated, and over the main entrance
was the inscription, " Fort Wicked." Entering the fortress,
we found a long adobe cabin, one part of which was occupied as a store, well stocked with groceries, canned provisions, and liquors. A bearded man, with a good-natured
but determined air, asked us if we would stop for breakfast. It was Mr. Godfrey himself, the builder and defender
of the fort, which is known all along the Platte as " God-

frey's Ranche." Here, last fall, he, his wife, and " another man," withstood a siege of two days by three hundred Indians, who finally retreated, after losing seventeen of their number. Mr. Godfrey boldly announces that he will never surrender. He is now well prepared, and the rumors of a new Indian war do not give him the least anxiety. He is "bad medicine" to the tribes of the Plains, who are as cowardly as they are cruel. The stable and corral are defended by similar intrenchments.

We had breakfast after an hour's delay, and then set forward for Julesburg, which was still some eighty miles distant. Daylight revealed the Platte on our left — a narrow, winding, muddy stream, with no timber on its banks. On either side the same bare, brown plain rolled away to the horizon ; streaks of sandy soil made the road toilsome to our teams, but as the stations did not average more than ten miles apart we made fair progress. The broad, well-beaten road swarmed with freight teams as the day advanced, and the condition of their cattle showed the excellence of the pasturage on this route. The brownness and apparent barrenness even of this portion of the Plains does not indicate a sterile soil, though it is undoubtedly more arid and sandy than any part of the Smoky Hill route.

The weather favored us beyond expectation. The day was overcast and delightfully cool ; mosquitoes and buffalo-gnats did not molest us, and every station we left behind added to our peace of mind. There was little to see beyond the fact that no part of this region is naturally a desert. The game has been driven away — even prairie-dogs are scarce ; — where there was timber it has been destroyed (fire-wood was furnished to the military post at Julesburg last winter at one hundred and twenty-seven dollars per cord !), and the first summer splendor of the flora had passed away. There were some wild sunflowers and lupines, and occasionally great purple beds of the *cleome*.

Sometimes the Platte, forcing its way through the long, monotonous waves of the soil, made for itself the sem- blance of a valley, with narrow lengths of fresh bottom- land and low knobs of hills ; but, on looking back on the day's journey, I can recall no single feature of prominence. It was one landscape all the way.

Until evening, at least. Then the sun came out and illuminated the barracks of Julesburg, the flag-staff, and flag. The buildings surrounding the parade-ground are of adobes — homely, but clean. The commanding officer's residence, of the same material — a French cottage, with mansard roof — is actually beautiful. We halted long enough to exchange a few remarks with the officers, and to be assured by them that there was no immediate danger of an Indian attack ; then we pushed on to the village of Julesburg, where we found supper, a two-story hotel nearly completed, a store and billiard-room ! I perceive that speculation (which is another name for civilization) is anticipating the Pacific Railroad.

We now passed out of Colorado into Nebraska, having made just half the distance from Denver to Fort Kearney. This was a matter for congratulation ; but the second night was coming on, and we had little hope that fatigue would bring sleep. One of our passengers only was fortunate. He had the happy faculty of distributing himself, as it seemed, all over the coach, and remaining unconscious, while his head was in the way of one, his hips of another, and his feet of a third. During the day, by mutual ar- rangement and concession, we relieved our cramped mus- cles as much as possible ; when we settled for the night (a mere make-believe) this was no longer possible, and the season of suffering began. Except while the horses were being changed at the stations, I do not believe that I slept at all. The desperate attempt to do so produced a dim, dazed condition, wherein I heard the constant roll of the wheels, and felt every jolt of the coach.

On Wednesday morning at daybreak we halted for breakfast at Alkali Station, a dreary adobe building in the midst
of a dreary landscape, which had not yet shaken off the
gray night mist. From this point the country began to
improve. The attempts of the Platte to establish a valley
of its own gradually succeeded.   There were marked lines
of bluffy hills on either side, green bottom-lands, now and
then imposingly broad, willow-brush along the river-banks
and on the scattered islands, and at last clumps of cotton-
wood trees. We still traversed streaks of sand, still drank
alkali water; but the road was alive with teams, and there
were grazing and supply ranches at intervals of four or
five miles. Here and there new adobe buildings were
going up. We saw red cedar logs, which the people informed us came from valleys in the rear of the bluffs; and
there was evidently no agriculture, simply because it had
not been tried.

The loneliness of the Plains was now so invaded that I
could only realize with difficulty where we were. We
passed mile after mile of great freight wagons — some of
them carrying four tons weight and drawn by six yoke of
oxen — of emigrant wagons, where the sunburned women
and wild-looking children were stowed among the piled
household goods, — there was no end to them. At noon
the wagons, under the direction of a train-master, were
" corralled " in a half-circle, the oxen turned loose on the
bottoms, and the teamsters — except those detailed as
cooks — took their ease in the shade between the wheels.
They appeared to be scattered portions of a single hun-
dred-mile-long caravan. The ranches were well supplied
with those articles which the strong and rather coarse taste
of these wagon-men demand: whatever their quality may
be, the prices are superb. Mr. Beard bought a small tum-
bler for seventy-five cents !

Before we reached Cottonwood, which is half way between Julesburg and Fort Kearney, the scenery became

pleasant, in spite of its sameness. The valley expanded
to a breadth of ten miles, and every winding of the Platte,
which here divides into several arms, could be traced by
its picturesque lines of timber. On the coach from Omaha
we found Colonel Chivington (of Sand Creek memory),
who gave us the welcome intelligence that the railroad
trains were within sixty-five miles of Fort Kearney. All
the passengers had their heads tied up, to keep off the
buffalo-gnats ; yet we were not molested in the least. At
Cottonwood, the bottoms of thick green grass, the clumps
and lines of timber, with the first appearance of the ash
and elm, were a delight to the eye. Here we got a capital
dinner, and the water began to lose its alkaline taste.

All the afternoon the landscapes of the Platte were
broad and beautiful. The accession of the north branch
gave the river a majestic breadth and sweep ; the valley
became fifteen or twenty miles wide, between bluffs which
now rose high enough to make low, blue headlands in the
distance. In some glens on the right we saw red cedar.
Here, at least, there is a fine field for agriculture : I doubt,
even, whether irrigation will be required. I had not expected to strike the fertile eastern belt of the Plains so
soon. It was a warmer counterpart of the rich French
lowlands, lacking only the grace given by centuries of
human habitation.

We rolled off the fourth hundred miles from Denver
during a third painful night, and at six o'clock on Thurs-
day morning drove into the village of Kearney, a mile or
two west of the fort. The stage was just ready to start
for the end of the railroad, and the local passengers ·in
waiting grudged us time for breakfast. The crossing of
the Platte, they said, would take from two to three hours,
and we should have trouble in reaching Lone Tree Station
by six o'clock in the evening. The station agent, however,
was on our side, and we snatched a hasty refreshment before departing for the ferry in an open, jolting wagon.

There were twelve hundred Pawnees encamped near the fort, and I should have visited their camp had it been possible. I only saw that Kearney is already a smart little village, which will soon be a town, and the centre of a splendid agricultural region.

The Platte is here a mile wide, its broad yellow surface marked by a thousand shifting currents and the ripple-marks of sand-bars. Two crazy little skiffs were moored to the bank, and in these it appeared we and our baggage were to be transported; another wagon far away on the opposite bank awaited our arrival. There was a pair of short oars in the boat, but the ferryman, instead of taking them, deliberately stripped to the skin and jumped into the water. We were advised to follow his example before taking our seats, but we only partially complied, retaining shirts and coats to ward off the scorching sun. The other boat being similarly prepared, we commenced the transit, which is unique of its kind.

If the Missouri pilot learns a new channel with every voyage, our Platte ferryman had even less dependence on his route. He chose his course entirely by appearances on the surface, avoiding both the sand-bars and the deeper portions, for we stuck fast on the former, and drifted in the latter. His policy was to walk on the very edge of the bar, towing the boat by the bow. Sometimes he walked a hundred yards up stream, then as far down again, tacking and veering like a ship in a shifting gale. At one moment he stood in a foot of water and the boat sat fast; the next, he plunged overhead and clung, floating, to the gunwale, while a passenger rowed. In half an hour we were half-way across; then one of our company stripped and went to the ferryman's assistance. Between the two, we reached the opposite bank in about an hour; the second boat, which had meanwhile stranded, detained us half an hour more. Such is the Platte — the meanest of rivers!

It was a jolting old mule-wagon which was waiting for

us ; but a stage we were told would be found some five
miles further on ! Away we went in the clear, hot sunshine, over meadows of splendid grass, along the edges of
beautiful groves and thickets, past the corn-fields of pioneer
settlers, when, behold ! an islanded arm of the river at
least two hundred yards wide appeared before us. We had
not yet crossed all the Platte. This arm, however, was
fordable ; all went well until we reached the middle, when
the team stuck. The bottom being quicksand, the moment the wagon stood still the wheels began to sink. Out
sprang our ferryman, seized the tires, and urged until we
moved again. Then a whiffletree broke, and again we
commenced sinking ; the process was repeated several
times, and we were all on the point of taking to the river,
when a final desperate tug brought us over the last
channel.

Once in the stage, we rolled rapidly down the valley. I
was surprised to find settlement pushed so far westward.
From the time we crossed the Platte we were never out of
sight of corn and wheat-fields — and what dark, heavy, luxuriant grain ! No irrigation is needed, and there are no
finer crops east of the Rocky Mountains. The native
grasses are rank and thick as a jungle, and furnish an
unlimited quantity of the finest hay. Some of the farmers
have planted little groves of cotton-wood about their houses ;
and the rapidity with which they grow (six to ten feet in
a year) shows how easy it will be to reclothe these treeless
regions.

We were detained an hour waiting for dinner, and the
chances of our catching the evening train so diminished
that we presented the driver with a slight testimonial of
respect, in order to insure greater speed. The horses were
poor and the afternoon very hot, but we reached Lone Tree
before six o'clock, and were finally set down in the grass,
beside the waiting train, some minutes before its departure.
Here there was a saloon and two boarding shanties, which

are moved as the road moves. The track is already laid fourteen miles west of the Lone Tree, and is being extended at the rate of a mile and a half per day. Recently *two miles and seventeen hundred feet* were laid in a single day — the greatest feat of the kind in the history of railroad building ! The grading has already passed Fort Kearney, and will reach Cottonwood — half way from Omaha to Denver — by next winter. Who disbelieves in a railroad across the continent now ?

When the train started, and the fair sunset sat upon the grassy swells and far dim groves of the Platte, I gave myself up to the exquisite sensation of rest. Aching in every limb, and feverish from loss of sleep, the knowledge that our hardships were over, was almost as soothing as slumber. There were but few passengers on the train, and each of us enjoyed the luxury of a double seat, arranged as a couch, for the night. Daybreak found us within ten miles of Omaha, and at six o'clock we were set down at the hotel, in precisely three days and twenty-two hours from Denver.

12

XXII.

GLIMPSES OF NEBRASKA.

St. Joseph, Mo., *July* 27, 1866.

EXCEPT that vegetables are earlier and more abundant, and that one is a little nearer to fruit and New York newspapers, I do not find a great deal of difference between the civilization of Nebraska and that of Colorado. Omaha and Denver are places of about the same size, — the latter probably the better built of the two. From this time on, the former will increase more rapidly; but when the railroad reaches Denver, I imagine the balance will be restored. The people of Omaha are convinced that their place will be another Chicago; and, as they see six hundred buildings going up this season, we cannot so much wonder at their "great expectations." They certainly have a beautiful location — if the Missouri River were to be depended upon. The crescent hills, open toward the east, inclose a high, favorable shelf of land, upon which the city can spread for some time to come. It is three miles across to the Iowa hills, and the picturesque town of Council Bluffs at their feet, so that they who reside in the higher part of Omaha enjoy a much broader and more beautiful view than can be had from any other place on the Missouri.

I devoted the first twenty-four hours to absolute rest, after my journey across the Plains. Moreover, the weather was truly African in its dry, intense heat, making sightseeing so much of a task that I deserve some credit for seeing anything beyond what the hotel windows allowed. In the pleasant company of Governor Saunders and Mr.

Frost, of the Pacific Railroad, I visited the height on which
the Capitol stands, the sulphur springs, and the extensive
shops and works which the railroad company has erected
within the past six months. What the latter has accomplished is really amazing. There is now rail enough on
hand to reach Cottonwood, one hundred miles beyond Fort
Kearney; several splendid locomotives are waiting to be
called into service, the manufacture of cars has commenced, and the grandest basis is already laid for carrying
on the business of the road. The ties, mostly brought
down from the Upper Missouri, — whether of pine, elm,
or cotton-wood, — are *burnetized* to render them durable.
Some idea of the enormous expense of building the road
may be obtained from the statement that each tie, when put
down in its place, has cost the company from one and a
half to two dollars! The cost of bringing railroad iron,
locomotives, and machinery to Omaha is also very great, as
there is no rail connection with the East. None of the
lines through Iowa will be completed before next summer.

The same process which I had noticed in Kansas — the
gradual restoration of forests — may be observed here.
The hills and valleys around Omaha, wherever they have
been protected from fire, are rapidly being clothed with timber. Clumps of cotton-wood and evergreens — sometimes
small groves of the former — have been planted around the
farm-houses, which are built in dips and hollows of the
boundless grassy waves of the landscape.

The country is one of the most beautiful I ever looked
upon. A little more sandy, perhaps, than Kansas, but
equally fertile, it presents the same general features. I am
more than ever struck with the great difference between
this region and that to the east of the Mississippi. Here,
without very bold or prominent forms, there is none of the
wearisome monotony of the prairie, as in Illinois; no unsightly clearings, ragged timber, or swampy tracts, as in
Indiana and Ohio; but Nature has given the smoothness

and finish which elsewhere comes from long cultivation; and in twenty years from now both Kansas and Nebraska will appear to be older than any other States west of the Alleghanies. They have little of the new, half-developed, *American* air about them; but suggest some region of Europe, from which war has swept away the inhabitants.

I crossed to Council Bluffs, which has an ancient, substantial appearance contrasted with Omaha. The people insisted that *their* rolling prairies, behind the bluffs, were even finer than those of Nebraska, — which is scarcely possible. They (the people) have just awakened to the necessity of annexing themselves to the business world, and are now laboring to hurry the railroad through from Boonsborough. Some day, perhaps, the Missouri may leave the Omaha side of the valley and come back to them: at present, their distance from the steamboat landings is a great drawback. The settling of Montana, nevertheless, has given a new impulse to all the towns on the river. No less than sixty boats have gone up to Fort Benton this season.

On Monday morning I took the steamer for Plattsmouth, some twenty-five or thirty miles below, by the river. I should have preferred the land journey, but for a heat of 102° in the shade, a wind like a furnace blast, and stifling dust. While the boat was in motion, a barely endurable temperature was produced, and I enjoyed, here and there, some lively glimpses of valleys on the Nebraska side, that of the Platte especially being superb. Plattsmouth is nearly a mile below the junction of the rivers, — a pleasant little place of a thousand inhabitants. Nothing but the heat prevented me from spending the rest of the day and evening very agreeably there.

On Tuesday to Nebraska City, forty miles further, by the river. There is little to note on the way except the endless changes of the current, adding hundreds of acres to the meadows on one side, and undermining cotton-wood forests on the other. Nebraska City is not seen to advantage from the river, to which it presents its narrowest side, the chief portion of the place — which has seven or eight thousand inhabitants — lying in the rear of the bluffs. It is an active, lively town, in spite of a predominance of the Missouri-Secesh element, as I am informed. I found a very comfortable hotel, and was indebted to an intelligent German physician for a drive around the heights toward evening. The heat was still my great torment.

There was no boat down the river on Wednesday, and as I had an engagement at Brownville, twenty-five miles distant, I was obliged to have dealings with a livery-stable. The extreme of extortion in this line had been reached, I imagined, in Kansas. I was mistaken. For the team I hired (driven by an ex-Rebel soldier) I was obliged to pay at the rate of *eighty-five cents per mile !* This is double Colorado and treble California prices. I was unable to resist the outrage; for the liverymen of Nebraska City have a mutual agreement to swindle strangers, and do not interfere with each other's operations. This is one of the disadvantages of travel in the West. We are told that competition regulates prices: it does not. On the contrary, *combination* keeps them up. No people are so fleeced and flayed as ours. The law offers no protection, because our politicians fear to offend any portion of the voting classes. "They manage things differently in France."

Neither the consciousness of having been imposed upon (a mean, disagreeable sensation), nor the stifling heat of the day could prevent me from enjoying to the full the magnificent country I traversed. During the five hours I was upon the road I never lost the keen sense of surprise and admiration which I felt on climbing the first rise of land after leaving Nebraska City. The wide, billowy green, dotted all over with golden islands of harvest; the hollows of dark, glittering maize ; the park-like clumps of timber along the courses of streams ; the soft, airy blue of the dis-

tant undulations; these were the materials which went to the
making up of every landscape, and of which, in their sweet,
harmonious, pastoral beauty, the eye never grew weary
Not even when the sun burned with the stupefying fierce-
ness of noon, and the vegetation seemed to crisp and
shrivel in the fiery south wind, did I wish to shorten the
journey.

Brownville is a small, but pretty town, with a decided
New England atmosphere. By the time I reached it, I
had decided that this should be my last day of mere sightseeing, and my last evening of lecture, in such a temperature. I turned away from the enticements of Pawnee, and
other interior districts, and resolutely set my face toward
home. There was no boat the next day, but a stage for St.
Joseph (between eighty and ninety miles distant) the same
evening; consequently a splendid moon, with neither heat
nor dust, for a considerable portion of the way. At eleven
o'clock I said good-by to the friends who had made my
short stay so pleasant, and, making a virtue of an inevitable
fact, decided that the night was too beautiful to be spent in
slumber.

The records of the United States Land Office at Brownville show that seventy-one thousand acres were entered in
the district during the quarter ending June 30. As two
thirds of this amount were taken by actual settlers as homesteads ; as the other districts of the Territory show very
nearly an equal growth, and as the business of the present
quarter, so far, keeps pace with the last, it is easy to estimate the increase of population for the year. It cannot be
reckoned at less than fifteen thousand, making the present
population of the Territory about seventy-five thousand.
When the splendid agricultural capacities of the country
are better understood, the ratio of immigration will increase. Nebraska cannot much longer be kept out of the
Union by A. J.'s one-man power.

The night-journey was delicious. There was no other

passenger, and I rode with the driver, a Union soldier from
Massachusetts, (how different from my Rebel of the day
before!) for the sake of society. The meadows, thickets,
groves, and grain-fields near at hand were clearly revealed
in the moonlight, but beyond them the scenery melted into
a silvery indistinctness. The signs of dawn came only too
soon, for with the first light of day I knew that the dewy
freshness of the air would be lost. I still had an entire
day of heat before me.

We stopped for breakfast at a place called Rulo (the
true spelling would be *Rouleau*, after the first French settler), and then pushed onward toward the Kansas line.
Across a bottom of almost incredible fertility, then a ferry
over the beautiful Nemaha River, and we left Nebraska
behind us. An Indian Reservation came next, and the
sight of two gayly dressed squaws on horseback, and two
naked boys trying to catch a pony, seemed to give a totally
different character to the scenery. It became again the
rich, free wilderness.

During the day I had several fellow-passengers, — a gentleman from the Cherokee Country, an intelligent and glo-
riously loyal Missouri lady, and several specimens of the
local population. The road ran some distance inland from
the river, climbing long swells whence there were out-looks
over ten or fifteen miles of magnificent country. All this
region is being rapidly settled. Villages — the sure sign
of permanent occupation — are springing up here and
there; neat, substantial farm-houses are taking the place
of the original cabins; and hedges of Osage orange are
gradually creeping around the broad fields. When I first
saw the bottoms of the Kaw and Smoky Hill Fork, in
Kansas, nearly two months ago, it seemed to me that such
extraordinary beauty and fertility must be exceptional;
but, last week, I found the same thing repeated on the
Platte, all the way from Cottonwood to Omaha. Now I
find it in the region intermediate between the two rivers,

and from what I hear of the valleys of the Neosho, the Republican, the Big and Little Blues, the Nemaha and Loup Fork, I am satisfied that what I have seen is the ordinary, average type of all this country. I consider Kansas and Nebraska, with the western portions of Iowa and Missouri, as *the largest unbroken tract of splendid farming land in the world.*

No one of us will live to see the beauty and prosperity which these States, even in their rude, embryonic condition, already suggest. The American of to-day must find his enjoyment in anticipating the future. He must look beyond the unsightly beginnings of civilization, and prefigure the state of things a century hence, when the Republic will count a population of two hundred millions, and there shall be leisure for Taste and Art. We have now so much ground to occupy, and we make such haste to cover it, that our growth is — and must be — accompanied by very few durable landmarks. All is slight, shabby, and imperfect. Not until the greater part of our vacant territory is taken up, and there is a broad belt of settlement reaching from ocean to ocean, will our Western people begin to take root, consolidate their enterprise, and truly develop their unparalleled inheritance.

Travelling all day in a heat of more than 100° in the shade — the seventh day of such an extreme temperature — I hailed our approach to Elwood, opposite St. Joseph, with inexpressible relief. During the afternoon we met a great many emigrant wagons, carrying " poor whites " from Missouri, Kentucky, and perhaps Tennessee, to lands of better promise. The lank, brown men stared at us from under their wild, bushy hair, with an expression of ignorant wonder ; the mothers, with their four to six small, tow-headed children (usually " one at the breast "), sat uncomfortably upon piles of antediluvian furniture, and patiently endured heat, flies, and dust. All of these people were but one degree removed from pure barbarism, and their loyalty must have had its root in instinct rather than intelligence.

If we could diversify the course of emigration, it would be a great blessing to the country. A current from the North to the South, with a counter-current from the South to the North, would "reconstruct" the former Slave States more solidly than any political measure. At present, the movement is too much one way; and nothing shows the narrowness and blindness of the Southerners so much as their continued enmity toward the very class of men they most need.

At six o'clock this evening I reached the Missouri, and crossed to this place. Here I am at one of the termini of railroad connection with the Atlantic coast, and may consider my travels at an end. Here the picturesque ceases, and the tedious commonplace begins. So here I close my communication with my readers, very much more fatigued by my experiences than I trust they have been in the reading of them, and yet more refreshed and invigorated than the kindest of those who have followed me can possibly be.

THE END.